Flight from the Russians

A German Teenager's World War II Ordeals

Flight from the Russians

A German Teenager's World War II Ordeals

Johanna Cotter McCloskey

Johanna Cotter McCloskey

as told to

Margaret G. Bigger

ABB   A. Borough Books

ISBN-13: 978-1-893597-08-2

ISBN-10: 1-893597-08-3

Library of Congress Catalog Card Number: 2005928519

Printed in the United States of America

COVER PHOTO: Original oil painting: "Flucht, 1945," which depicts the bloody flight in dirty snow from her hometown just before the siege of Breslau in January, 1945. (38"x42") By Johanna Cotter McCloskey. Copyright 1997.

ABB

A. Borough Books

Charlotte NC

FOREWORD

While editing *World War II: It Changed Us Forever* and, in 2003, *World War II—Hometown and Home Front Heroes,* I became fascinated by true war stories told by the people who lived them. In the first book, Agnes Hostettler had been a teenage daughter of a Jewish mother in Nazi Germany. She wrote of having met Hitler at the 1936 Olympic Games before he ruined her life. She escaped to Switzerland just before Kristallnacht.

What about other children in Germany? I wondered. Yes, I knew that many Jewish children shared their parents' fate. But what about those of the Aryan race? Could they have lived a normal life while their Führer waged war on other countries and then committed suicide, leaving his people to suffer defeat alone?

While taking one of my Recalling Memories for Posterity courses sponsored by the Charlotte Writers Club, Christa Mercer, a young child during the war and, more recently, Johanna McCloskey, a teenager who fled the raping Russians, gave me a glimpse of what I was seeking. I believed each had a story that the general public would find fascinating.

Christa's collection of short stories (*German War Child - Growing Up During World War II* published in 2004) and now Johanna's recollections and journal notes written during her flight bring alive the era that we still struggle to understand. Both give us enlightened insights of family life so normal one day and bizarre the next.

Johanna's plight was far more dramatic, for her lifestyle switched from luxury to extreme poverty. Imagine leaving a lavish home in Breslau with gorgeous clothes and jewelry in your closet, fine Persian rugs on the floor and multiple cars in nearby garages and, within less than a year, becoming ragged and homeless with no belongings and no idea whether the rest of your family might be as lucky as you—alive! This teenager averaged up to 55 kilometers a day walking until she began hopping on trucks and trains, first to get away from the Russians and then to find someone to take her in and help her find a job.

You will shiver with her in the snow, suck your breath with fear, experience hunger pains, exhaustion and loneliness and also pray that somehow she will locate her family alive.

But then, readers, you can *rejoice* with her when Johanna finds her own freedom and a new life.

- Margaret G. Bigger

ACKNOWLEDGEMENTS

My special thanks go to my sister, Kiki Skiebe, for loaning me her journal and telling parts of her story that I had never heard. I am also grateful to:

* The Parche family—Herta, who filled me in on family stories, Christoph, who provided a detailed map of Germany, and Andreas, who helped us determine which town is in what state.

* Eva Brinck Hancock, who now lives in Australia, for sharing her personal story and pictures.

* Annelies Hahn Blosser for explaining the Brinck family background.

* Jeremy Russell, a fellow artist, who used his skills to produce an outstanding photo of my painting for the cover.

* Jerri Gibson McCloud, an author herself, who painstakingly prepared my vintage photos to fit into my story.

* Margaret Bigger, my editor and new friend.

THIS BOOK IS DEDICATED TO
MY SONS, WHO HAD
NEVER HEARD THIS STORY
BUT ENCOURAGED ME TO WRITE IT:

TOM

ROBBIE

PETER

DISCLAIMER

I have worked diligently to verify the statements of fact throughout this narrative, but the passage of time dims the memory and sometimes leads to error.

To the extent that there may be errors herein, I ask the reader's patience and understanding.

CONTENTS

Hanna's parents, Helene and Georg Skiebe
Breslau. 1923.

INTRODUCTION

Like soldiers on both sides of the war, I repressed my most traumatic memories until the 50th Anniversary of D-Day, when the media magnified the horrors of that period of history.

It angered me that no one, to my knowledge, had ever written about what we of Silesia experienced from the siege of Breslau until all the Germans had been deported—and the chaos that followed. A teenager then, I had kept a journal of my flight. Amid all the anniversary "hype," I rushed to retrieve that ragged little book from my safe-deposit box. That night I sat in bed and tried to read my scribbles. The pencil I had used had become lighter and lighter and, over the years, the pages had grown darker. As I struggled to decipher it, the feelings of extreme loneliness and despair returned. I could not continue.

My three sons knew some of my background, as we had visited my father in Frankfurt in 1964. Then in 1993, Charlotte, North Carolina and Wroclaw, Poland became sister cities. I could not believe it! The largest city in the region where we live was linking with my former hometown (Breslau before the Russians and then the Poles took it over). Immediately, I volunteered to work with the committee. Soon, my husband Buddy and son Peter traveled with me, the rest of our delegation and Mayor Richard Vinroot on our first official visit. After performing our duties, we viewed what was left of my family's apartment houses and my grandparents' home. Six years later, my son Tom, his wife and son, my sister Kiki and I went to Wroclaw and then to other cities to visit German relatives. I made a point to see my favorite Pole, Anna Jalinska, who became like a daughter after we met in Wroclaw. In 1997 with Sister Cities, we saw the Pope in the very same building where I had seen Hitler!

It was Tom who insisted that I go to Christa Mercer's 2004 book-signing in Davidson. The author of *German War Child* told her story, and someone asked that I tell mine. Her editor, Margaret Bigger, suggested that I take her Recalling Memories for Posterity class—and now she is *my* editor.

My family knows nothing of my flight. Frankly, I remembered very little until I photocopied and enlarged the pages of my journal. Later, I suddenly thought of the cyanide capsule and, at another time, the Nürnberg trial I attended.

Even my sister Kiki did not know of my ordeal (nor I of hers) until we discussed my book and then she mailed me *her* journal!

Hanna, Helene and Kiki Skiebe
Breslau, 1932

I. The End of an Idyllic Life

More than a year before this night, my father had told me that Mother did not have much longer to live, but that did not make reality any easier.

Her kidney disease was in an advanced stage. Her body parts were disintegrating, and she would be in distress every 15 minutes. Someone had to be with her all night to assist. Her devoted nurse, a nun, had to leave to care for the ailing Mother Superior, and Tante (the German word for aunt) Friedel had been with her the night before. She had asked me to be the substitute care-giver.

Knowing that I could be a heavy sleeper, my mother tied a multicolored scarf onto my wrist to yank whenever she needed me. That worked most of the wee hours, but, although having been seated in a chair next to her bed, I suddenly awoke with a start on her chaise lounge. Tante Friedel was tending Mami.

I felt *so* guilty, especially when the doctor came in to give her morphine, our priest administered last rites and other family members gathered in her room. It seemed so unreal.

My grandfather went crazy with anguish that morning of July 4, 1941. Three times, in earlier years, last rites had been administered to him, yet he was alive, and his daughter-in-law, a young woman with two children and so many possibilities, would not see another sunrise.

Our mother died peacefully with a smile on her face.

Grandfather rushed to our room, grabbed my sister's prayer book and put it into Mami's hands.

Soon, they were bringing in a casket, which would be taken to a chapel at the graveyard, where she would lie in state for a day before the funeral.

Even at 15, almost 16, I was scared of dead people. It seemed spooky viewing my sweet mother with eyes closed, encased in a box. My sister, three years younger, was stoic like a stone. I shed enough tears for both of us.

11

Yes, I knew this day would come. Actually, I had expected it sooner.

At age 35, Mami had an operation on one kidney, but soon after that, she was okay. That was in 1933, when I was 8. In 1940, the kidney disease resurfaced, and she was hospitalized for 100 days. We visited her daily at St. Joseph's Hospital. She had a lovely room with huge windows. Holding up a silver framed hand mirror just so, she could view the Oder River from her bed. She did have some constant company. Her pet parakeet, the very verbal Hansi, lived there, too.

Mami resting at
St. Joseph Hospital
Breslau. 1940.

One afternoon, my neighborhood friend Susie Peters and I hopped off our bicycles, secretly rented a rowboat and set out on the river in front of the hospital.

My diminutive classmate and I skimmed downstream, but trying to get back seemed to be beyond our strength with the current going against us. As we struggled, the boat wobbled and bobbled, and I was afraid Mami would see us.

Fortunately for us, she never noticed.

Truly, my mother should have been hospitalized longer, but my dad contracted scarlet fever.

At age 40, he was admitted to an isolation ward in a bungalow of the University Clinic, and Mami decided that she needed to be home. Soon afterward, my little sister, only 7 years old, caught the same contagious disease with fever and a nasty rash. She was also put into isolation at a children's hospital. We could only wave to her, as she and other young patients screamed from their windows.

Mami was not bedridden but spent much of her time in a chair reading, crocheting, writing letters and seeing that I did not get in trouble.

Sometimes, she played with our parakeet, talking to the pet perched on her finger. She taught Hansi to say "Papi, old

Bummler (one who drags his feet coming home)," and "Mami, give me a kiss." When I was around, Hansi would chirp "Hanna, lazy girl." While playing in Mami's room, Hansi liked to flutter down to a mirror and talk to himself.

Soon, my father's cousin, Friedel Miserre Schoss, came from Berlin to help out. A widow with an attractive French tan, dark hair and eyes, she was very chic and up-to-date and did a good job running our household and supervising the personnel. She was not our aunt, but we always called her Tante Friedel.

Use of cabs during the war was limited. Only because she was ill, Mother was allowed to take a taxi once daily to check on our father.

While there one morning, she ran into the woman she knew her husband had been fooling around with.

Käthe Prietsch, who worked as a secretary at a department store, had been introduced to my father by his best friend. Also a married man, that guy had tired of this ebony-haired French Moroccan free-wheeling hussy and passed her along.

Devastated, Mami rushed home, took pills, pills, pills, climbed into her hot tub and waited to die. The window to her bathroom was covered with wrought-iron bars and the door was locked, so it took hours to get her out. We children were involved in after-school activities and did not hear of it until the crisis was over.

At last, she was in her room, where her doctor cared for her. Then came the nun who had been nursing her to take over. When Mother felt better, we gathered around, and she started laughing—but no words would come out. Then she got serious. For a whole week. she was literally speechless.

A devout Catholic, our mother expressed deep regrets, knowing that what she had tried to do was a serious sin.

As her speech returned, Mami's kidney condition worsened. Her hair thinned and receded, her delicate skin grew whiter.

After my father and sister recuperated from scarlet fever, he brought in a renowned homeopathic physician, who had offices in London, Prague and Berlin, to treat Mother. Dr. Mrochem mixed and administered his own remedies for such notables as Neville Chamberlain. Whatever concoction he gave her prolonged her life another year. Mami's hair started to grow back, her cheeks blossomed without rouge and her eyes, those loving hazel green eyes, glowed with hope.

Even so, her fate was inevitable.

And I had thought the biggest change imaginable was when my baby sister interrupted my comfortable life.

After my sibling was born in January 1929, Mother stayed four weeks in the hospital, surrounded by relatives, other visitors, flowers and boxes of candy. Once again, my father wanted a boy, perhaps another Georg Hermann Skiebe. He had wished I was one, then Mother had a miscarriage of the male he desired, so he would have to settle for Christa Stephanie, and she became his favored one. Not yet 4 years old, I couldn't pronounce her name, so I called her Kiki. Soon everyone else did, too—except when someone spoke harshly to her, then it was "CHRISTA!"

Names in my family did vary from time to time. My paternal grandfather's last name had been Skiba, but he changed it to sound more German than Polish. Joseph had wanted to change it again to Skiberg, but my father, his only—and quite spoiled—child said "No!"

I knew him as Opa (a name generally used for a grandfather) and I called that grandmother Omi, a sweeter term than the usual Oma.

Everyone called me Hanna, although my given name was Johanna Dorothea Katharina Skiebe. Dorothea was for my German grandmother, Anna Dorothea; Katharina, for my mother, Helene Katharina Piskorek, and my Polish grandmother, who spelled her name Kataryna.

That grandmother Kiki and I called Babscha. I saw Babscha only twice a year when we visited her in Krotoczyn, Poland. In her little black hat and black garments to the floor, she would listen attentively to what I was telling her, nod and say the Polish word for "Yes, yes." As she was then a widow, I never met my mother's father, Jan Piskorek, born in 1845 and died in 1922. All of that family with 11 children were redheads, from the darkest auburn to strawberry.

As a boy, Opa learned to be a sausage maker as an apprentice in Berlin. After three years, he became a journeyman;

14

Hanna in Omi's ample lap. Breslau. 1926.

three years later, a master of that craft. He and a friend bought tickets to America, but he told his pal, "I have to go see my mother first."

He traveled back to Ostrowitz to tell her goodbye, but she wouldn't let him go. Of her children, all tall, blonde and blue-eyed, Joseph was the smallest and probably the favorite. Every one of his relatives was tall. His uncle, Peter, who was his age, visited us one time. Peter was a head taller than Opa, about 5'8" at that time.

After missing his chance to go to America, he linked with another friend, Hermann Kusche. Each of them chose Breslau to start up a business. Hermann opened a butcher store; Joseph, a sausage-making factory. One weekend, Hermann took Joseph to his family farm in Pollogwitz, where Joseph met his friend's sister Anna Dorothea Kusche, the reason we call him Onkel Hermann.

Breslau was the major city of Silesia in the east of Germany. Throughout the years, it belonged to Poland, Austria, Hungary and Prussia. Even the French Army occupied it for several years on their quest to conquer Russia, which never happened.

When the Germans tried to get rid of this occupation, gold, jewels, and other valuables were collected to buy weapons to free themselves from the occupying French. This drive was called "Gold gab ich für Eisen," which meant "Gave gold, got iron." Jewelry made of iron became patriotic symbols. One hundred years later, my grandmother bought a piece of that iron jewelry during World War I for the benefit of the Red Cross. I have it still.

World War I brought more hardship and misery to this war-torn country. France took over the southwestern part (Elsass-Lothringen); Poland acquired the eastern part. Large regions of Germany became Polish, and the people there would speak both languages in those instances. Czechoslovakia became a separate country. Those were hard times for this nation, with no jobs, food, clothing or building materials.

At the age of 17, my father, Opa and Omi's only child, volunteered for the German Army. He became a war prisoner in France. At war's end, his parents were greatly relieved to have him back. He had hoped to go to college and become a veterinarian, but his parents couldn't understand why he wanted that, when he was the heir to a very successful business!

Opa had done well in his sausage-making enterprise and owned five or six apartment buildings. Breslau, by then, was a metropolis of more than 600,000. As the chief Silesian market, it was known for its iron foundries, machinery, textiles, paper and furniture. A university, technical school and seminary drew scholars to the region. Our city also featured beautiful buildings, many with spires brushing the clouds and reflecting in lakes, ponds and the Oder River.

In 1923, when my parents married, they moved into one of my grandfather's apartment houses on the lovely Dom Insel (Cathedral Island) with many ornate churches, including the famed twin-spire Cathedral of St. John the Baptist, as well as a botanical garden and the technical school within a few blocks.

On the corner of Sternstrasse and Hirschstrasse, it took up much of a block and housed Joseph Skiebe Wurstfabrik, their company, in the deep basement and part of the street level. The animals were butchered every Monday on the other end of town, but the meat was processed and smoked at the factory in huge ovens. Heavy iron doors kept the aromas from penetrating the atmosphere.

Although the building housed 26 other families in small, two or three-room flats, theirs and my grandparents' apartment filled almost the entire second floor.

When our family grew, Opa and Omi moved upstairs. The two apartments were merged, giving us three bedrooms, a family room, a rarely-used kitchen, dining room and library. Another kitchen, where most of the food was prepared by servants, was on the first floor.

Both families had plenty of household help. Two laundresses came the first of the week to wash all our laundry, including white coats and aprons worn by the factory workers and the cotton runners that protected our fine rugs. They boiled the clothes in kettles in our attic. Everything was hung on lines to dry until Wednesday, when the ironing ladies came. On Fridays, two women cleaned our home from top to bottom, even if it was not dirty.

Kiki and I had a happy and privileged childhood, which I did not realize then.

Not only spacious, our home was well appointed with room-size Persian rugs in the living room, dining room and library and smaller ones in a couple of the bedrooms.

Our family room, where we spent the most time, was lively with the songs of Mami's birds (canaries and parakeets), the tail-swishing of Papi's guppies and the begging and barking of our boxers of which Moritz and Barbel were the most notable. Barbel took on a rather haughty attitude, perhaps because she was the victor of the 1929 Boxer Show in Berlin.

Although every room had fine furniture, the Herren-zimmer (literally translated men's room, but library would be more accurate in English) featured a smoking table from India with an elaborate metallic top like a frame over beautiful wood. In chairs around it, guests could relax and smoke. Papi generally took only a few puffs of a cigar a day.

Mami never smoked at all. Her treasures were locked away in a fancy bookcase with a glass door.

All of us loved books, but behind that door were records and genealogy papers somehow proving that her family descended from aristocrats. News had come from some village verifying heritage from the 1600s. Mother entered that information into a journal in her beautiful script. I begged to read it.

"No, Hanna, you can read the records when you're old enough," Mami told me sternly.

I never saw them.

I might have been tempted to unlock that cabinet door when no one was looking, but I did not because of an incident of my early childhood. Always a nosey child, I tried to unlock Omi's cabinet with straight pins. Omi had to get a locksmith to open it, and I got in trouble.

Beyond the three paneled windows, flowers of the season bloomed in window boxes, and double glass doors led to a balcony. A rubber tree stood as tall as I at age 10 next to the balcony door. Often, Mami would purchase long-stemmed fresh chrysanthemums for her favorite floor vase.

More treasured than those, her rhododendron traveled a long way to reside at our house.

When I was 8 years old, we surreptitiously brought that bush back from Babscha's yard on one of our visits. "Smuggle" is a better word.

As vegetation was not to be transported across the border, we walked from the railroad and left the rhododendron beside the border police headquarters, where they sifted through our suitcases and bags. When they finished, Mami picked up the plant and went over to the German guardhouse to go through a similar routine, the potted bush just outside the door. Papi was waiting for us in his snazzy Mercedes and whisked us and her precious rhododendron away.

Actually, we had a garden on the outskirts of town, a ten-minute walk from our apartment house. Depending on the time of year, dahlias, lilacs and asters decorated patches of gooseberries, green onions and/or climbing beans. On a piece of lawn and in a nearby sandbox, Kiki and I played with our girlfriends.

Sometimes, Ulla Richter, a girl who lived in a neighboring apartment, joined the fun. (Although Ulla was three years and one day older, I called her my "bosom buddy.")

As Papi raised boxers, there was also a kennel for the dogs on the property.

Music was always around us. Radio, singing, whistling and dancing made for a lot of happiness. In our dining room adjoining the library, a Grundig radio entertained us from a side table and my father's upright piano in the corner awaited nimble fingers, large and small. Kiki and I played piano, harmonicas and, later, accordions, but she did not have my music passion. I performed with a private accordion orchestra of 45 kids.

Until she married, Mother had rarely played a piano, so she learned on the same one we did. Even so, she could not keep in tune with her voice. Our music-loving Papi, on the other hand, had melodies in his blood. He—and we girls—could stay right on pitch.

Only once did I have a musical malfunction. At my school, St. Ursula, I was to lead a chorus performance of three classes: the one ahead of me, my class and the one behind. My parents proudly sat in the audience awaiting my directing debut. During rehearsals, the music sister had given me the pitch for the first note. I started one group, then the next one began a half note down and the third came in on another note from that. But at the concert, the music sister left me on my own. Extremely nervous, I began with the wrong note. Then I saw the sister raising her arms. Moments later, she rushed in and took over. I was mortified.

Mami loved the opera and attended local performances every two weeks. Papi accompanied her to the lighter operettas, plays and concerts but did not care much for Richard Wagner's operas.

All of us had fun hopping around the house whistling. Papi would come in from work whistling.

 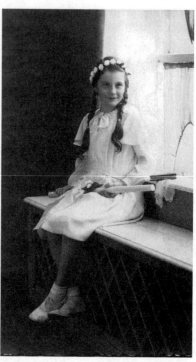

Hanna's first day at school, with traditional "school cone" full of candy. Breslau. Fall, 1932; Hanna, dressed for her first communion, with the traditional candle. Breslau. June 2, 1935.

As they were members of numerous organizations, our parents attended many balls. At times, Mami, my nanny and I would gaily dance room to room.

Both of our parents were artistic. Mother, in fact, became a passionate photographer. With her Voightländer, she snapped family shots of outings and vacations.

Among her handicrafts were crocheting, knitting and embroidering elaborate tablecloths. She taught me how to crochet. A perfectionist, she never overlooked one of my crocheting mistakes.

I loved nursery school and kindergarten, because I learned how to basket-weave and to fold and cut paper, making fancy doilies.

My introduction to art was by my father. Whenever I was sick, he would bring in a tray to my bed. On it would be paper, colored pencils and postcards. He challenged me to copy newspaper or postcard pictures in color. That was fun, and I began drawing cartoons of international figures like Chamberlain, Churchill and Hitler. Art is now my passion.

Papi's passion was automobiles. At different times, he owned a Chrysler, Horch, Mercedes, a NSU Fiat, and numerous others as well as Ford and Chevy trucks for his business.

Every now and then, he would rush in all excited to tell my mother, "Hella, I've found the most wonderful car!"

"Yeah?" she would say, lacking enthusiasm.

"Yeah!"

"Do we *need* another car?"

Her questions were in vain. He always bought what he wanted. He parked his excess automobiles in a building behind an apartment house owned by our family that adjoined our apartment's property. The particular personal car he drove daily stayed in our backyard garage.

Mami really wanted to learn how to drive and took classes for three months.

In Germany, you had to be able to repair a car as well as steer it. That was the hard part.

One afternoon, when we preparing to go to Pawelwitz, a lake that was a 20-minute ride from Breslau, she turned to my dad. "Let me drive the car."

ABOVE: Mami, Papi, his prized Chrysler, Hanna, Omi and Opa on a mountain outing. Circa 1928. BELOW: Opa preferred real horsepower all his adult life. Breslau. 1918.

"Get your own. It will only cost 500 Marks," he replied, but he relented.

As she approached the lake and was turning to park, an argument broke out between them. He yanked the steering wheel away and our Horch ended up halfway into a ditch. We were screaming. He was shouting, and Mami was unhappily trying to defend her actions. She never did live out that dream.

But learning anything new was in her blood. Reading, reading, reading. Sometimes she had three books in progress. Never a college graduate, she could speak six languages: Russian, Polish, Czech, French, English and German. After high school, she lived with her sister in Breslau, while working as a kindergarten teacher and taking courses in accounting. She had a job in that field and her own apartment when she met Papi. For much of their married life, she served as a bookkeeper for our family's businesses.

While my grandfather was buying and renting out apartments, Papi was buying and managing movie theaters, although both were still in the sausage-making business. The largest, the American Movie Theater, was in Breslau. Four others were in small towns nearby.

By that time, the sausage factory at Sternstrasse 35 employed about 25 people. They also owned two stores that sold smoked sausages and delivered to butcher stores all around Silesia. The company was best known for Kielbasi.

Our other joys were hiking and swimming.

On most Sundays, we drove out into the country, where we met with relatives and friends, took long walks and later stopped for coffee and tortes. These get-togethers were always happy with good food, music and dancing. But, my sister and I were too young to have the fun our older second cousins could enjoy, like teenage jokes and sports. The adults talked about their businesses and families or played cards.

Weather permitting, we went swimming every day.

Quite often, Papi drove us to Pawelwitz. On a particular day when I was 13, he flung me into the water. In his usual manner of treating me like the boy he never had, he gave the order: "Swim across the lake."

My unathletic friend Susie didn't know how to swim,

so she chatted with my mother and sister. Meanwhile, tiring fast, I wanted to pause for a moment at a sandbank in the middle of the lake.

"C'mon, c'mon. Let's go!" he hollered from over my shoulder.

When we got to the other side, we could not stop because it was private property. I was pooped but had to just turn around. He kept urging me on with "You can do it!" until I finally could get out of the water. All I wanted to do was find something to eat and do my homework.

Other days, I took a streetcar to the Hallenschwimmbad (like a Y), where I donned my one-piece bathing suit, a dark wool uncomplicated garment with a round neck and straps, and swam laps in a heated pool.

We spent four or five weeks every summer at Göhren, a resort on the island of Rügen in the Baltic Sea. At the Göhrener Hof, our family rented rooms on the second floor, enjoyed meals in the restaurant and relaxed on the beach at our own Strandkorb (a basket-like woven rush structure with an awning and pull-out hassocks). At a private part of the beach, where our sand castles could not be touched by other tourists, Kiki and I would lie in the sun, swim or play with toys, water balls or a ring ball. This rubber ring, like a little tire, could be caught with a hand in the hole and then flung back with a twist and a flair.

Just a few months more than three years apart, my younger sister and I enjoyed many of the same activities, but we were quite different actually. She was like a little bird; I was a curious cat. Everybody always catered to her or felt sorry for the darling little sweetheart. Quiet but playful, she stayed busy with her dolls or a playmate. Conversely, I could not help but be rambunctious. I always wore shoes with flat heels and took long steps.

Once when I stomped into the house noisily whistling, my mother showed her annoyance by throwing a set of keys at me. Yet, I represented her side of the family with my fire red hair, far brighter than her "orangy" strawberry. Kiki's hair was nearly white at birth but soon turned Skiebe blonde and, as she grew older, ash blonde.

Happy holidays: LEFT TOP: Billa and Papi carrying Kiki. Göhren. 1932. LEFT BOTTOM: Hanna, Billa, Kiki and Papi at the beach. Göhren. 1932. RIGHT: Mami and Hanna at Binz on the Baltic Sea. 1932.

From the age of nine months on, I had a nanny, which is still a puzzle to me, especially since Mami nursed me for eleven months. My mother was so sweet and so kind, but she was "well-heeled," and I guess it was just expected.

Billa seemed genuinely pleased to be with us, and over time, I figured out why. Her father had married Mami's older sister after his wife had died in childbirth. Billa Ramnitz had been the youngest motherless child. As her stepmother soon had her own little daughter to raise, she may have resented young Billa.

Like her father, Billa also enjoyed music and had taken piano lessons for ten years. When my mother lived with her sister before she married, she had noticed that Billa did not appear to be happy.

Children then began high school at age 10 and, by 16, could start an apprenticeship. That is when Mami invited this lonesome and misunderstood brown-haired 16-year-old to live with us as my nanny.

As expected, she was strict, but our nanny kept us busy, entertained and safe. Vivacious only when dancing, swimming or fast-walking, she seemed to have daily headaches. Every day, she emptied an little envelope of powder into a glass of water and swallowed it. I couldn't wait to be old enough to do that. It looked so chic.

One day when we were at Göhren, she and a male acquaintance, whom we called Onkel Hamann, were taking one last dip in the Baltic Sea, when she developed a cramp in her leg and could not swim back. What a drama! We worried, but watched Onkel Hamann drag her out, help her dry off and get her into our car to go home. He was her hero—ours, too.

Her smiles encouraged me, but when her disapproving blue eyes stared at me, I knew I was in trouble.

Billa, Hanna, Mami and Kiki playing cards after a picnic.
Hartenberg. 1931.

A drill sergeant, she made sure we did our homework, kept us clean, neatly dressed and well-behaved. She was particularly strict about my practicing on the piano. Once, she locked me into my room for punishment. I became frantic, scared I would never get out.

My impression of her was a disciplinarian, perhaps because I more often acted naughty to get attention. Kiki, a meek child and easier to handle, thought of her as loving. "She carried me all the time," Kiki recalls. Perhaps that was because Kiki had to have a serious operation when she was 6 years old, thus needing extra attention.

Mother, meanwhile, lived her own life, like other women in her position, entertaining and being entertained. Even so, she always found time to kiss us awake, say good-bye lip-to-lip and then welcome us with a homecoming kiss.

Every day, Mami's lovely red hair was combed and styled by the hairdresser who owned a salon downstairs in our building. Her pretty little hands were kept supple and her nails perfect with translucent polish by the manicurist downstairs. Those tiny feet, which could wear only a mannequin's shoes, were tended to by a pedicure lady, who stopped by on a regular schedule. A masseuse came once a week.

Behind the closed door of Mami's room, we could hear "smack, smack, smack" of hands slapping on skin and wondered what was going on in there. *Was that meanie hurting my Mami?*

Our mother always wore hand-tailored clothing, with outfits for every occasion. A mere 5'3", Mami would have some of her clothes altered for me, when she tired of them or gained a little weight. And when I could no longer wear them, they were passed on to Kiki or sent to poor relatives' children in Poland. Even with our luxuries, nothing was wasted.

Likewise, my father's clothes were hand-tailored. He preferred English coats, Scottish wools and overcoats lined with fur for winter.

From time to time, he would travel alone or with his pals to attend auto exhibitions in Berlin or boxer club events wherever they were held.

Of course, he took all of us to Göhren annually.

I once asked, "Why do we have to go there every year?"

"As long as you're here and I'm paying for it, this is where we go," he replied in a tone only a father would use.

On one of those long road trips from Breslau to Berlin and beyond, where we caught the ferryboat to ride two more hours to the island, we could feel unusual excitement in our capital city. It was the summer of 1936, during the Olympic Games. No, we did not get tickets for any of the events, but we observed athletes and their supporters in various costumes and colors, celebrating the occasion.

Our maternal uncle from America, whom we called "Crazy Josef," and his wife Antoinette, however, had crossed the Atlantic Ocean to see the games.

It was Josef who invited Mami to visit him in his adopted country. She took this trip-of-a-lifetime the very next year. For four weeks in May, she toured New York and Washington, DC.

An adventuresome woman, our mother truly wanted to fly by Zeppelin, a type of rigid airship that was all the rage then. At the last minute, she decided to go by ship, the S.S. Europa.

Good plan. The trans-Atlantic dirigible Hindenburg crashed and burned in Lakehurst, New Jersey in May, 1937!

While Mami traveled, Kiki and I attended a private summer camp, Kinderheim for about six weeks on the island of Wangeroog.

Supposedly on a kid's vacation, we children were under very strict guidance as if we were at school. Actually, I happily swam, played ball games, ran, socialized and sang. But 9-year-old Kiki did nothing but cry.

Most of the campers were either from Berlin or Breslau, so we girls divided into separate clubs. We nicknamed them the Berliner Quadratschnautzen (Berlin bigger mouths). They branded us Bresläuse (Breslau lice).

When Mami returned from America, bearing gifts, all of us met her at the train station.

As she stepped off the coach, I swished my long pigtails and shouted, "That's not my mother!" I meant it. "She's not a German woman!" I added for emphasis.

ABOVE: Tante Antoinette, Kiki and Onkel Josef in the Skiebe home. Note tile stove on left. BELOW: Tante Antoinette and Kiki in the library. Note floor vase in front of Kiki and bookcase ("safe" for treasures) behind. Breslau. July, 1936.

The woman who tried to hug and kiss me had unbecoming dark penciled eyebrows, bright red lipstick and scarlet fingernails. I refused to kiss that obscene lipstick.

We returned home to unwrap presents. I was not impressed, but Papi showed great delight when he saw what she had found for him: a windshield with little wires inside. When attached to his regular windshield, it could be heated. No more snow or ice to wipe off!

Despite all these advantages, my first 15 years had not been perfect.

Papi professed to be a Lutheran, but Mami was a Catholic, so we were taught by very strict nuns, first at St. Anna for grades one through four, then at St. Ursula. For small infractions, our hands were slapped with a wooden pointer used by our instructor. If we did not pay attention or caused a problem, we could expect a paddling.

Considering that he was a well-loved only child, who probably never felt a whack, Papi did not hold back on me. Of course, I could be a little devil at times. Usually, he would spank with his hand, but once, he broke a broom on me, when he caught me reading instead of doing my homework.

My mother displayed her temper with me on occasion, too. While in Pollogwitz, I secretly donned her ocelot coat to consort with Omi's family's fascinating pigs, geese, chickens and pigeons. When I came back in the house, she whack, whack, whacked my face with uncharacteristic anger.

The worst thing she ever did, for which I have a hard time forgiving, was not to allow me to join her tennis club. Only Mami and a cousin had joined to learn how to play and then enjoy the competitiveness and comradeship. Papi had other interests. But, I really really wanted to become skilled in this exclusive sport of the times. Mami called the other members "snooty" and did not want me to get sucked up into their culture.

The worst thing I ever did to her was unintentional.

On a pond two blocks away from our home, she and I were ice-skating together when I was 9. My foot hit a crack and I slipped. She skated over to steady me and fell hard on the ice. Screams of pain told everyone around us she was seriously injured. Indeed, both her tibia and fibula were broken! She could not get up. "Don't touch me! Don't touch me!" she squealed at people trying to help by bringing a sled.

"I'm sorry, so sorry!" I wailed with great remorse.

At last, a doctor came and arranged for her to be transported to a hospital.

I felt terrible. My guilt intensified when Omi later swore that her fall in 1935 contributed to Mami's problems with her only remaining kidney.

Could it be that, because of me, I would never again feel my sweet mother's hugs and kisses?

My life would never, ever be the same!

The Skiebe apartment house. Hanna's family had the corner apartment with the balcony. Breslau. Circa 1940.

Charcoal drawing of Adolf Hitler
by Johanna Cotter McCloskey. 2005.

II. Hitler, Our Country's Hero

As soon as I turned 10, in 1935, I delightedly joined the junior division of the Bund Deutscher Mädchen (League of German Girls), the female version of the Hitler Youth. School then ran six days a week. If we joined, we did not have to go to classes on Saturdays. That was the incentive, but it was generally expected that everyone would be patriotic and join. Furthermore, we kids were curious.

Very similar to Girl Scouts, BDM sponsored outdoor activities like hiking, bodybuilding and sports, but we Jungmädchen (Young Girls) also sewed little shirts to be donated to underprivileged babies and practiced new crafts. Once, we were given plywood to draw on. With small saws, we cut out our designs, then painted and fashioned them as wall hangings.

Another time, we each went dashing around with a little can to collect donations for needy children.

All of us thought we really looked spiffy in our uniforms. Our navy blue skirt had one pleat in the front and slit pockets on each side with a button at the top of the slit. With that, we wore a white short-sleeve shirt, a black triangular scarf and a mustard-colored jacket with four buttoned patch pockets. A leather woven knot, which slipped on the tie, matched our sturdy brown shoes.

An active teenager, I enjoyed marching alongside the Oder River, exercising, running and jumping. We played lots of sports, especially volleyball and Brennball (similar to baseball).

My friend Susie Peters was the only one who never joined the BDM, but it did not strain our relationship. Her divorced mother had to work, but her father and grandparents, who lived in Berlin, were quite wealthy and took her on fabulous trips in the summer. During the school year, she was among the very few who had to be in class on Saturdays.

Before Hitler's ascent to power, Germany's economy had crumbled. Although we were what others would consider well off, those were difficult times for everyone around us, and eventually for our family.

In the 1920s and early '30s, even those with jobs could not make a decent living. The unemployed had to sweep the streets or shovel snow for a daily hot meal from the "Goulaschkanone" (a portable large kettle for cooking with four wheels to push around the different streets). I can still see people standing in lines for their portions.

When inflation began to become a serious problem, Opa sold one of his apartment houses. Initially, he received half of the purchase price. The value of the Mark plummeted and, by the time he got the second half, it had lost value so drastically, that he could buy "only a pack of matches," his way of describing the pittance he received.

Before she was married, while working as a bookkeeper, Mami got paid every day. She and co-workers would hurry out and purchase whatever they could before their Marks were devalued more.

In her locked cabinet in our library, where she stored those genealogy records, was a mountain of old Marks, which had no value.

Fortunately, my family never experienced hunger. My grandparents worked very hard from 4:30 a.m. until 10 p.m. in their Wurstfabrik overseeing employees. They still could provide jobs, because people in Silesia still needed to eat. And those sausages were delicious!

After January 30, 1933, life for the masses began to change. Adolf Hitler had come into power. All able-bodied people were put to work. Coal miners, whose pay had been too measly to feed their families, earned better salaries. The poorest farmers could make a decent living. Hitler soon was building autobahns and creating jobs. He saw to it that cars (Volkswagens, at 500 Marks) which most families could afford were produced.

Soon, swastika flags were hanging out of windows all around Breslau. Ours hung off the balcony. Both of my parents were very patriotic. My father joined the Party. He never wore a uniform but showed loyalty with a lapel pin (a little round symbol with a swastika in the center and writing around it). Our family made great contributions, especially sausages, for the needy. And we invited students from the university or the technical school for daily meals.

In a nearby neighborhood, red Communist flags had been displayed long before the swastika. Radical women shouted from windows at anyone in a brown uniform. On voting days (which were frequent), females yelled at people wearing a "Ja" (yes) pin, indicating Hitler loyalty. We kids stayed away.

But one afternoon, we were coming from a circus and had to catch a streetcar that passed through that part of town and stopped at the edge of it, where we were to get off. That neighborhood was surprisingly quiet. A police car's lights flashed silently. Then a cop lifted a megaphone and shouted, "Get off the streets! Close your windows!" No one else was in sight.

Almost at our streetcar stop, Kiki, Billa and I were terrified. The stop was a block away from our home. *Should we keep going? Make a run for it?* Together, we leaped off the trolley and raced to a crevice in a building wall. Looking both ways and seeing no one, we sprinted to an alley, then a doorway until we reached our own apartment double doors. As soon as we got upstairs, our mother warned us: "Don't go near the windows!" We never heard any more about it but later saw bullet holes in building walls and blood splatters on the sidewalk. That, perhaps, was our first glimpse of what might loom ahead, but to us it was just an incident.

In March 1936, Hitler delivered a speech in Breslau to thousands in the Jahrhunderthalle, at that time the largest round building in the world. We stood for hours in front of my aunt's house to see him in a procession to the Jahrhunderthalle.

Finally, we went inside to get some water and returned to wait some more. At last, he came into view in a beautiful black Mercedes convertible. His hand was up higher than his head, his elbow out greeting us. We, in rows five people deep, returned his greeting with an enthusiastic "Heil, Hitler!" Not a negative word was spoken, only shouts of appreciation. Many more automobiles with dignitaries followed, with secret police on the running boards for protection. I got goosebumps screaming and yelling with the crowds. It was like Caesar coming by, and we could actually see our leader's face!

Another time, when he came to our city, I attended the speech with my BDM. We were given prime seats near the front on the Jahrhunderthalle's right side. Thrilled by the occasion, I was soon bored by his speech, for he was never known to be brief.

When Adolph Hitler spoke, his country listened. Loudspeakers blasted his words from street corners whenever he made a speech. Our family sat in the dining room to hear it on the radio. Again, I would get bored as he raved on and on for two hours. Even Mami grew weary. She would bring in a pencil and paper and write shorthand and scribbles.

A major event for Breslau in 1937 was the Sängerfest. Competing cities sent their best singing groups for contests. A highlight of the fest was a parade along our Sternstrasse, featuring the contestants in their ethnic costumes led by flag-bearing marchers. Swastika signs festooned the parade's path.

A similar parade marched down the same street one year later for the Turnerfest (athletic competition). At that time, the Germans in Czechoslovakia had not been "rescued" (by the Nazis), so, as they passed our windows, that group was chanting in their marching cadence: "Lieber Führer mach uns frei, hole uns aus der Tschechei." (Dear Leader, make us free and get us out of Czechoslovakia.) Tall, handsome, athletic men in short pants and matching gray shirts marched on with pride.

Usually, I slept like a bear, but on November 9th of 1938, I awoke to loud sounds of "bang, bang, pow, clink, clank, tinkle"—pounding and breaking of glass. I ran to my window to see the Sturmabteilung (SA, a Nazi paramilitary group known as "brown shirts") smashing the front of the pub at end of the block across the street. In the commotion, I heard yelling and cursing from the perpetrators.

The pub had displayed the obligatory "Jude" (Jew) sign on the window. Yes, it was the infamous Kristallnacht, the pogrom against Jews instigated by the Schutzstaffel (SS storm troopers or "black shirts"). By ten o'clock the next morning, Jewish-owned stores and many private apartments were demolished. A large number of the people who, by law, had been required to wear a yellow star indicating their religion had disappeared.

Turnerfest parade outside Hanna's window. Breslau. 1938.

The next morning, our class at St. Ursula was scheduled to take an airplane flight over Breslau. While aloft, as we flew over the center of our city, a huge fireball burst into the sky. The largest synagogue in Breslau had been blown up! Neue Synagoge burned for hours. Smoke spread over the city like a pall.

My father owned a fine apartment house in another part of town on Victoriastrasse, where the wealthiest Jews resided. He never mentioned whether his building met the same fate.

Shortly before Kristallnacht, Papi was upset with Mami one day, because she had bought a fine set of china from an elegant store with a "Jude" sign. "Don't you know you might have been hurt?"

Surely, the store-owner who made a profitable sale would not have hurt her. He meant the Nazis.

Many of our doctors had been Jewish. I was unaware if they, too, disappeared, but I know now that doctors, medical workers and patients at the local Jewish hospital were evacuated that night and taken to Buchenwald.

Some Jews remained, I am sure. Our "soap man" was Jewish. When rationing went into effect, the only soap we could buy at the market was sandy and coarse. But, the "soap man" we had always bought from continued to stop by for awhile and sell us his fine product.

Eventually, just about everything was rationed: meat, milk, sugar, shoes and even clothing. Because citizens could not buy as much meat as they wanted, the sausage business slumped. With our ration card, we bought the food allowed from stores in our neighborhood and then, like most everyone else, bartered for the rest.

Poles also became objects of Nazi hatred and brutality. My mother considered herself a German and never joined the Polish Association, so I was never aware of that situation. Thank goodness, for I had other worries.

My mother's death in 1941 was heart wrenching, but 1939 was almost as traumatic for me.

That spring, Kiki and I felt abandoned by our grandparents and the nanny who had cared for us all our lives.

In May of that year, Omi and Opa bought a peaceful

lovely home from the town mayor of a suburb of Kanth, about 20 miles outside of Breslau. Our dear grandparents with whom we shared so much of every day were leaving.

Oh, how we would miss them! Both were huggers. Omi had a large lap that we could snuggle in when she read to us. For Omi, we were her reason for living, and all four of us felt her love. Leaving her only son and grandchildren must have been as hard for her as for Kiki and me to lose both of them.

Opa fooled around and kidded me a lot. Like the time when I was about 4 years old, he rolled up a newspaper. "See this cigar?"

It did not look like a cigar to me.

"Close your eyes." As I obeyed, he continued, "Hocus pocus, here comes a cigar!"

I did not believe him. Surely, he had pulled that cigar from his pocket. I let him know I was not easily fooled. That never stopped him from trying.

He used to take us for rides in his shiny carriage pulled by two black horses so stunning that the mayor borrowed them for parades.

Neither of them could drive an automobile, so they would not be coming to see us very often. Opa would be riding the train some Saturdays to check on the factory, but from May on, we would be visiting them on weekends, usually Sundays.

There were some advantages: Omi always greeted us with cakes and other wonderful goodies. And we got all our fresh fruit and vegetables from their big garden. As soon as we arrived there the first day, I ate all the fruit and nuts I wanted. But, when everyone in the family was supposed to help harvesting later that afternoon, I was up in the attic reading.

From time to time during the school break, Omi would let me bring a girlfriend to spend a week or two. As Susie was not very athletic, I took another friend, Irmgard Lassak. Her father was a dentist, and she had two brothers, which meant she did more outdoor sports. We would pedal our bicycles to the train depot, throw them on the coach headed for Kanth and enjoy the short ride. As we were climbing back on our bicycles, we admired the stately castle of General Blücher within sight of the Kanth station.

Omi always spoiled us. We loved to sleep late, and she would come in at nine o'clock to coax us up, gently calling me "Hannele" (an affectionate version of my name) and describing a delicious breakfast that awaited us. At ten o'clock, she would be back, enticing us with another sweet too good to resist.

A great new toy was the dumb waiter from their kitchen below to the dining room. Did we ever ride it? You bet! It was our private elevator when no one was looking.

Behind their home beyond the extensive garden (long not wide) was a cement swimming pool with brick trim. The pool was never filled. Only in winter did we play there, skidding around on a thin layer of ice, which had settled in the bottom after cold weather.

Near the rear of their property was a garden house next to an expanse of grass where we could play sports.

Most surprising was the Pelztierfarm (a mini-zoo) with brick walkways and trim iron fences. But my grandparents' only animals were chickens, pigeons and our boxer Bonko, who stayed in another part of the garden.

They had a maid, Gisela, and a gardener, an old man who came from the neighborhood. Gisela told me all about life. I told her I was *never* going to get married.

My father owned the property next door, with a garden full of nuts and fruit and an empty spot where his retirement house would go. Perhaps this would be where we could all call home someday.

Billa, who enjoyed dancing in her free time, had been dating Albert Assmann, a neighbor who lived across the street from our apartment house. She was 30; he, 25, but they fell in love. On June 2nd, only a few weeks after our grandparents left us, Billa married and moved away.

Within several more weeks, we got another nanny from the Sudetenland. Bianca Schramm was much too sweet, a "tweety bird," quite the opposite of our drill sergeant, Billa. As we were 14 and 11, there was not much need for this 20-year-old, who probably had never done this job before, so she did not stay very long.

It was that same year that I decided to assert my independence by going to a beauty parlor, having my pigtails cut off

40

and getting a permanent. Mami knew my plan and worried about my father's reaction. Truth of the matter, there was nothing he could do to change it. He just didn't speak to me for four weeks.

It was obvious that our government had major military plans. Already, they had annexed Austria and reclaimed Rhineland, Sudetenland and the rest of Czechoslovakia. Then on my 14th birthday, August 26, 1939, they mobilized an army unprecedented since the First World War. Young men were drafted, and everyone who had served in the military under a certain age was called back. Poor Billa, her husband got drafted only two months after their wedding.

On September 1, 1939, when Germany invaded Poland, the war that civilians anticipated began. What much of the rest of the world did not realize was the brutal chaos that the people in that region had experienced since that part of Germany became Poland after World War I. Germans' farms were burned. The Polish committed atrocities on Germans who chose to remain there. We considered the invasion retribution and an act to take back what was part of our country. But Great Britain and France declared war on *us* two days later.

Soon, we were hearing horrible war news from newspaper boys yelling headlines, talk on the street and reports on our Grundig radio. I was frightened. Omi told me about the First World War and that it had lasted four years.

"Four years!" I repeated, shocked. I could not imagine a war that would affect four years of our lives.

Even before this monumental event, some were becoming apprehensive about Hitler, his motives and plans. My own mother, before her hospitalization, invited a lady friend into our library to whisper about their fears. Mami probably felt concern because of her Polish relatives. Most of the population, however, believed that, if Germany were to win the war, Hitler would become a god, for he would see that everyone had jobs and a better life, as he had done for his own country.

Another positive side of the reclaiming of Poland was that there were no more borders, no checkpoints, as we were reunited. Babscha was an old woman in an unimportant town, which the soldiers marched right through.

For my Onkel Antek, who had a farm and many kids, the future was not so calm. He and other Polish workers were being transported by railroad to the east. While the train was underway, he jumped—and was shot mid-air.

As we knew times were hard there, we sent packages with clothes and salami, candy and whatever we thought could make Babscha and her other grandchildren happy. And we continued our visits without the hassle of border searches. The later trips were by train. If Mami and Babscha spoke of the war or retribution involving the rest of our family, we children never knew it. They spoke only Polish.

At school, we soon began learning present history. That is, every morning, our teacher placed pins on a large wall map, noting where the German Armies were, and we would discuss that region: Denmark, Norway, Holland, Belgium, Luxemburg, France, Yugoslavia, Greece and more. When our soldiers were in Russia, we learned that they were up to their hips in flood waters. In winter, they nearly froze in extreme Russian snows, but some crawled atop tile heaters in abandoned homes to sleep. We also heard that, whenever they came out of the field, they had to be deloused three times.

In addition to the usual high school courses, we had to take French for six years and English for four, like the schoolgirls before us. France had already become a part of the Third Reich. Would we soon have England? It *did* seem possible.

As in other countries, even children did something for the war effort. Our accordion band played a benefit concert for wounded soldiers, who were trucked in from various hospitals.

By 1941, when rationing was instated, my father and grandfather worried about the business. The volume of sales was down, and the deeper we got into war, the fewer able-bodied workers were available.

Foreign workers began coming in from France, Poland and, later, other conquered countries such as Holland, Belgium, Latvia and Estonia. They and late-middle-aged Germans, too old to be drafted, took over the vacant jobs. The company provided living quarters on the fifth floor, six to an apartment, when they had no local family. The French were the best—so nicely behaved, never rowdy. And they did not steal.

42

During May 1st celebration with Skiebe personnel: Lotte and Hanna in front of Papi's Horch. Sponsberg. Circa 1937.

Papi's real interest was in his movie theaters. He had to take a three-to-six month course to learn the technical side of how to operate a theater and run the projectors.

After the Japanese attack on Pearl Harbor, when the Americans entered the war, Papi began to doubt that Germany would win. He used to say, "If the U.S. gets involved and Ford Motor Company starts making aircraft, the sky's going to be black with planes."

Meanwhile, nighttime became especially dark. The old gas lanterns on the streets were adjusted not to burn brightly, and we had to pull black shades over our windows or get reprimanded sharply by watchmen, whenever air raid alarms sounded. Lights on automobiles, streetcars and the numerous bicycles around town had a covering to allow only a slit of light.

Day and night, hundreds of freight trains ran east on every track with boxcars of supplies such as arms, ammunition and uniforms and open cars loaded with tanks and military trucks. Those trains returned for more and went back again.

Once I turned 14, BDM met in the evening. I saw that

as an opportunity to go to the movies. Someone, probably with the BDM, told my mother. That was one of the few times I saw her angry, except when I skipped piano lessons without her knowledge.

As the war dragged on, my father reluctantly gave up his beloved automobile collection. They all got drafted! So he bought a new Fiat, which used less gas. Even so, he later was not allowed to drive it because there was no gas, so that cute little car went up on blocks. Then *it* got drafted! By the end, all he had was a small wooden wagon with a little white horse.

Only a few months after Mami died, our father brought Käthe Prietsch into the business as an apprentice at one of the stores.

How could he? This was the woman who caused my mother to attempt suicide! Every time I thought of her, I recalled the night my parents were invited to a ball. Mami was all dressed up ready to go, when my father came home.

"Where do you think you're going?" he asked her in a gruff voice.

She stammered something about the ball.

"I'm not going with you! Look at you!" he stormed.

Our mother was beautifully dressed in an elegant gown. We cried and cried, Mami in her room, Kiki and me in ours. We found out later that he had attended the ball with Käthe.

Tante Friedel had stayed on for awhile after our mother's death. She knew Papi would not live alone for long, and I think she had her eyes on him. She gave up. He was not interested in her. His eyes were on Käthe.

Fortunately, I did not have to watch their relationship develop for very long. As soon as I finished school in 1941, I had to do my year in a household.

Even though we had two maids, each and every girl had to work in someone's household. It was a government-required obligation. For girls, it was known as the Pflichtsjahr (duty year). Young boys, before they became old enough for the draft, were expected to do Arbeitsdienst (work duty) wherever needed, even building bridges. They wore brownish uniforms. We girls only had to wear an apron. When working in the garden, I hung a mosquito net over my head.

Meanwhile, women were doing men's jobs: operating streetcars, delivering mail, driving taxis and such to keep the home front as normal as possible.

I had until then no idea how to wash dishes or make a bed, and I couldn't cook. So things were not easy for me, but I soon learned at Dr. Winkler's home in Maltsch.

There, I was responsible for three young kids (two boys and one girl). We played games and went for walks, and I kept their clothes and rooms clean. The boys were already in school, but I had their preschool daughter full time. I seldom used the strict attitude of Billa, as I was little more than a child myself.

This was a general practitioner's household, and I sometimes had to help in the practice in his home office. Always, I sterilized instruments and assisted with washing out patient's ears.

That house had two examining rooms. The other was for Dr. Winkler's wife, who was a dentist. Mostly, she treated foreign laborers, especially the French.

Thank goodness we had a maid, who cleaned the rest of the house, cooked and helped out wherever needed. Mrs. Winkler liked to cook, too.

When I got a few days off, I went home. Soon after I got there, my father announced, "My friend Käthe is coming today. I want you to meet her."

I definitely did not want to meet that dark-eyed, dark-haired witch, but I decided to make the best of it and suggested that I fix a steak for dinner. Our family enjoyed roast beef, but I do not remember ever having steaks. I had learned how to fix them and wanted to show off.

When I had finished, and Papi, Kiki and Käthe were waiting for me, I could not make myself go into the dining room.

My father came to get me. "Come on, Hannele."

I was shaking with too many ugly memories, but I followed him in. My first impression: *She's fat! Smoking like a fiend!* Nothing about her made me like her, even the stylish hairdo—combed back, with "curly-cues," obviously set by a hairdresser.

45

When I met her family, I was not particularly impressed. They lived in a lower middle class suburb, and yet her mother seemed sweet in a subdued way. Having been cowered by an abusive husband who had died, she seemed not to have any self-esteem. Käthe and her sister, Friedel, appeared to be opposites. The sister resembled my mother (red hair, very smart) and was likeable like her mother.

Our father's girlfriend undoubtedly took after her domineering father, a fact we determined a short time later.

For the wedding, I took off from work again just long enough for the festivities.

I had designed my own dress for the occasion and found a dressmaker to make it. Finding the fabric was not easy, but it was dark blue tulle over a lighter shade of taffeta with puffed sleeves, a tight waistline and a flared skirt to the floor.

Käthe was Catholic; Papi, a Protestant. They married in a Lutheran church in the center of town, and with that service, our life changed considerably. I was as upset as hell. For Kiki, life *became* hell.

I could go back to the Winkler household. Kiki had to become one of our stepmother's servants.

She would have liked to run away. Instead, she took her wire-haired fox terrier, Putzi, for a walk three times a day, just to get out of the house. Kiki only walked around the block, but it was her escape.

The new ruler of the house insisted that she dry the dishes, even though our family had hired help to do such things. From Kiki's point of view, that left no time for her to do homework.

For me, there came a new unpleasant surprise at Dr. Winkler's home. The strange thing was that this good family did not want me to leave after that year was over and I had learned a few things. But, then, if you stayed one more day, you were a maid. That was not my desire in life.

So my stepmother came to rescue me. That is the only nice thing she ever did for me.

I reported the situation to Käthe on the phone, and she offered to help. She came marching in like a soldier and demanded my release.

After a few private words with the doctor and his wife, she got her way and we left that house.

The railroad ride took four hours, that August of 1942, because of air raid alarms and stopping so as not to attract the attention of bombardiers. Sapped by the trip, we could not catch a taxi, as we were not wounded. So Käthe and I had to lug my suitcases to a streetcar stop. At that time of night, they did not run very often. We arrived home relieved but in the middle of another alarm.

My state obligation over, I considered my future and decided to take some courses in shorthand, typing and accounting at a business school for six months—or I would have had to work on a farm or in an ammunition factory.

At that time (late 1942, early 1943), Breslau had few bombings, but many an air raid warning at night. Our Luftschutzkeller (air shelter) was in the basement of our building. Throughout the city, doorway passageways were broken through the connecting walls to the next building and the next, so that citizens would not be trapped if a particular apartment house was hit.

My next job, beginning in the spring of 1943, was as secretary for a Wehrertüchtigungslager (defense camp) for Hitler Youth in the mountains. Again, the alternative would have been to work on a farm or in a factory.

For three weeks, groups of Hitler Youth from ages 15 to 17 came to learn to read maps and a compass, shoot guns, march and experience being away from home.

As secretary, I had to make out reports, type letters and keep schedules. It was a great job, because we were in session three weeks and off one. Then a new group of boys would come in.

My boss, the Lagerführer, Wolfgang Simms, was a military lieutenant, who had been wounded and could no longer fight. Very tall, he rode a tiny motorcycle around the camp and the little town of Habelschwerdt.

All of the 16 Ausbilder (trainers) were also wounded military men. Others at the camp included a Red Cross nurse, a female administrator, the kitchen maids and a Polish handyman, who stayed drunk all the time.

LEFT: Staff members at Hitler Youth Camp. Hanna, center back row. RIGHT: Trainers playing a bottle game. Habelschwerdt. Circa 1944.

We called him Panje, when we needed him to make repairs and, in winter, keep the fire in the furnace burning. But to me, he was the "dirty mop," because he slept in the boiler room, rarely washed and stunk like a skunk.

The teenage boys slept on bunk beds in a huge factory building, where they got relatively good food for that period of the war, usually a soup with vegetables, potatoes and noodles and occasionally, some kind of meat.

One day, though, I was enjoying the soup when I saw worms swimming with the noodles. Bravely, I kept on eating. I was too afraid to say anything.

We also had plenty of eggs. The Behörde (government authorities) required anyone with normal-size chickens to give extra eggs not needed by the immediate family to help feed others. (When that regulation came out, my grandparents got bantam chickens, too little to qualify.)

Some of the boys passionately loved the heel-clicking, gun-shooting military camp. Others could not wait to get out.

I had a private room in a wing for females in one of the barracks with no shower. We had to bring in water and pour it from a pitcher into a basin. The showers were in the main building. Women went at a different time.

Herta Sindermann, the administrator, a moody old maid, did not like me. Why, I do not know. But she did seem to like Putzi, Kiki's wire-haired fox terrier.

I had brought the dog back from a one-week stay at home, because our stepmother was making life more unbearable for Kiki and complaining about the dog.

Putzi apparently enjoyed her new life too much, for she soon had puppies. I gave one to my co-worker, and suddenly she loved him dearly and became friendly to me.

Herta Sindermann, Putzi and Hanna. Habelschwerdt. 1944.

My trips home were not always pleasant.

After several medical procedures, Käthe had had a baby in April, 1943, a girl they named Edeltraut, soon to be known as "Trautel." Kiki was expected to be an unpaid nanny, while Käthe smoked and Papi ate chocolates.

Once, I brought home one of the kitchen helpers from Habelschwerdt. My stepmother bawled me out. "That girl: she doesn't belong." What she meant was that this person was not a doctor's daughter. No, she was my new friend.

Oftentimes, a man turns into a coward when dominated by a strong woman. That was our dad. And, although Käthe complained of how badly he treated her, she was, in Kiki's eyes, the culprit.

One night, when I was there, I could hear an argument through the thick wall that separated our bedrooms. Apparently, Käthe came in from the bathroom and moved a chair next to the bed. Papi stumbled into it. "Put it the other way," he said, indicating where my mother had always kept it.

His wife slapped him so hard I heard it. He tried to calm her, which only made her madder. Suddenly, she was climbing into my bed. "I'm not going to stay with him!" she hissed.

I took off for Kiki's bed and urged her to move into Omi and Opa's house. Grandmother really wanted her to come.

"No." She shook her head. "I want to protect Papi."

On another visit, Kiki, by then 15, was gone. Had she taken my advice? No, her class from school had been sent to the Eastern Front to dig ditches, so that Allied tanks could not cross. Those young girls and their teachers slept on straw in a farm home attic until the four-to-six-week job was done. By then, all denominational schools had been ordered closed.

Incidently, the nuns at St. Ursula had accepted Jewish girls, even after other schools rejected them. Then suddenly, they all left headed for America, England, Canada or Australia. These were children of the wealthier Jewish families of Breslau, who could afford to leave before Kristallnacht.

When refugees of German descent from Hungary and Romania began fleeing cruel Russian invaders, Papi defied the law and started listening to Bulgarian radio news reports.

He could have been shot!

As the war began enveloping Germany, supply lines were cut. Troops took priority, so food for its citizens became scarce. Never a problem for our family, the sausage-makers, it threatened the health of many others.

On a trip home, I heard from Kiki that my "bosom buddy" Ulla Richter, who had married and moved across town, was nursing a baby, but was short on nourishment for herself.

"Bosom buddies" Ulla and Hanna. Breslau. 1929.

I sneaked some food from our house and took it to Ulla.

Later, Kiki reported that the infant had become wrinkled and shrunk smaller and smaller until he died.

That broke my heart to hear. And, I am sorry to say that I never saw Ulla again to tell her.

It was in Habelschwerdt that I finally got to enjoy the company of boys.

At St. Ursula, a gymnasium (boys' school) was next door, but we were on different schedules. In winter, sometimes the guys would throw snowballs at us. I got hit on the shin once. And one might jerk a pigtail when passing me on the sidewalk, but that was about the only relationship I ever had with males near my age outside of the family.

In Breslau, the biggest social events for young and older teenagers were dance classes and the resulting society dances, but Mother never allowed me to go. She had met my father that way and found it too painful to consider.

While in my Pflichtjahr (duty year), the nice lady who ran the local general store in Maltsch had a son about my age. Horst and I met with a local bunch of guys and gals in their teens on Sundays at a restaurant. They all drank beer. I tried some but didn't like it much.

Fun at camp: LEFT: Two trainers ready to ski. Habelschwerdt. Winter, 1944. RIGHT: Hanna (center) with the nurse's sister and Susie Peters. Habelschwerdt. Summer, 1944.

My companions from the camp barracks and I often joined some of the soldiers at a little mountain restaurant with good food, singing and playing of cards. It was like a family room, hosted by the owners.

One time, while playing poker, I lost my whole month's salary. But Omi was sending me money all the time, so I never missed it.

In front of our camp was a river, where we swam and "puddled around" with boats and guys.

Another recreation I enjoyed in Habelschwerdt was at the shooting gallery. My parents competed in riflery. Our mother was a champion at festivals in Breslau and in Göhren. I took up the sport at Johannesfest, an annual amusement fest.

The only threat we felt in those mountains was from the Allied bombers, which began flying over every day at noon. In anticipation, a swarm of gray uniforms and caps, 160 of them, would make way to a mountain bunker with multiple caves before that hour. I joined them but always stood at the opening. There were no strategic targets to bomb in our area, so we became rather blasé about it.

Not one bomb fell, yet we never neglected to seek shelter.

We never ever knew what the next day would bring.

III. Flight to Safety?

In mid-January, I returned to Breslau. Everything had changed. No one was working then, only dreading a Russian invasion. All women, children, elderly and crippled men had been ordered out by Nazi Gauleiter Karl Hanke. Men and older boys capable of holding a rifle (the Volkssturm: People's Army) were expected to stay and defend their homeland: "work a miracle," according to Adolph Hitler's radio orders. Thousands of prisoners of war and compulsory workers from other countries had to remain and labor on.

Our historically picturesque city, with its stately churches and Hanseatic houses, now pock-marked by bombs and smoked by fires, faced an even worse fate. Flags of the Third Reich were flying above the rubble, although it was not yet January 30th, when the anniversary of Hilter's coming to power was celebrated. (Kiki's birthday was January 30th, and my dad used to say, "See, Kiki, those flags are flying for you!")

That January, Gestapo Chief Heinrich Himmler commanded troops and civilian patriots in East Prussia and Silesia, while our army was in full retreat from Czechoslovakia. But the Red Army, led by Marshal Koneff, would begin their invasion soon, encircling Breslau. It would become a death struggle, a "siege" they called it, that would last nearly three months.

My boss at the Hitler Youth camp got a transfer, so I put in for one, too. We were both assigned to Lüben in Silesia. From Breslau also, Wolfgang Simms, our Lagerführer, wanted to see his family first, so we traveled by train to our hometown.

The station was jammed, a madhouse of masses of people, some waiting, others rushing to catch trains before the dreaded occupation. Such a commotion! Yet exhausted children and old people were sleeping in all that turmoil.

Once on the streetcar, I stared out the window at crowds of what appeared to be refugees and then workers laboring as though nothing was happening. But on the streets, there were no cars, only military vehicles traveling east to west.

When I reached our home, I raced up to my room to pack a suitcase with clothes I thought I might need plus my favorite shoes, the last I had bought—red flats, handmade, from Czechoslovakia, square in the front, decorated with different colors. I would have liked to have taken a piece or two of the family silverware, but I was afraid that my father would be angry. I wrapped a cardboard box of family photos with string so that I could carry it in my hand. In my canvas knapsack, I packed toiletries and my ID. I would take a jacket but wear my heavy coat lined with Mami's ocelot fur, the fur of the coat I wore while helping to feed those pigs, geese, chickens and pigeons. My nickname for it was "the cat."

I spent that one night with my dad, not in our apartment, but in the basement because alarms sent us there.

Papi's assignment was checking for bombs that had not yet exploded. He had already saved our home, when a Brand-bombe (small bomb) had landed in the attic. He was credited with notifying the authorities fast enough to stop the fire from spreading into the apartments.

That was when he had moved some of our furniture and his precious collection of Persian rugs to the basement, where everyone remaining in the apartment house gathered and stayed together for comfort. The rest of our family was gone.

Papi had insisted that Kiki drive the wagon with Käthe, her sister Friedel, both of their one-year-old babies and necessary belongings to our grandparents' home or a nearby farm where a relative lived. Friedel's husband had just been killed in Romania.

That custom-made "flat back" wagon was the one that Papi used to replace his confiscated Fiat. Despite four brand new tires from that Fiat, their little white horse balked at pulling such a load. Kiki told us later that she had to get out, grab his reins and tug him down the road.

After the invasion of Poland, my mother's oldest sister's son, Stachu Siberna, had fled and came to my father to ask, "Can you get me a job?" In peacetime, he had been administrating huge farms, the property of Polish gentleman farmers. Papi knew of some land outside of Kanth which was owned by two elderly ladies who could use his help.

If our grandparents could not accommodate everyone, Stachu would find room for them at that farm.

My father expressed pessimism about our future. He worried that Kiki and the others never made it to safety. He told me that Breslau had been declared a fortress, and Goebbels had ordered the men and boys to defend it with forks and knives. We both despaired of the invasion but had to accept it and probably the death of all of us.

Papi could not stay all night, for he had to do his duty, and the bombing was intense after dark. But he was back the next morning to tell me goodbye. We kissed—and how! We had always been an affectionate family, but this was not a joyful embrace. Papi and I had a hard time releasing each other.

Chaos surrounded and invaded Freiburger Station. Frantic women and children and old people, who could not get out the day before, were pushing, shoving, burrowing into the crowd, some hysterically, some with a glaze of unbelief.

I was to meet Wolfgang there at 10 a.m. to go to Lüben, but I could not find him in the tumult. Refugees of all ages were crammed in every coach of every train in that station, wedged between the cars, hanging off the sides and clinging to the top. Had my lanky boss hopped on another train?

No time to search. I pushed my way to the first train that I knew was heading west and jumped on a coach. More and more and more crowded inside, squeezing, squeezing me until I thought, "I can't breathe!" Had I been near a door, I would have jumped out. I was suffocating to the point that I would have climbed over those shoulders and hats if I could have moved from that spot. Heaven help the young children among all those legs!

By early afternoon, I had gotten off at Lüben and hurried to a school, which was the Hitler Youth camp headquarters there. I was relieved to see my boss.

A day or so later, we heard by word of mouth that six Russian tanks had broken through the line and had crossed the Oder River. We were on the west side of Oder and knew it would only be a matter of time before the Russians arrived, and that we must escort our boys to safety as soon as the sun came up the next day.

Actually, the youngsters and their leaders left later that morning, but at 2:30 a.m. on January 26th, I started walking with Wolfgang's sister Eva and a nurse and her fiancé, a wounded soldier with a wooden leg. Before we left, each of us swigged some Kartoffelschnaps (potato schnapps) for courage.

Eva Simms and I quickly bonded as best friends. Tall like Wolfgang, Eva was far more beautiful than her brother was handsome, with blue eyes that contrasted with her dark hair. She and I shared much in common: our hometown, similar ages and interesting insights about my boss. Eva was Lutheran, as were my father and grandmother. More than anything, we enjoyed each other's company, even in unpleasant circumstances.

This was one of the worst winters in Silesia, with temperatures as low as six degrees Fahrenheit. In waist-deep snow, we took off, step by labored step. We took turns pulling a small sled from the camp on which we had piled my mother's leather suitcase decorated with American stickers, my knapsack, their luggage and assorted packets. In all those carefree winters of sledding as a child, I never thought of using one for anything but exhilarating fun.

Never seeing a road, we headed in the general direction of the town where we hoped to link up with the campers. Our eyes saw only snow and sky. Our minds concentrated on fear of the unknown—or maybe six thundering Russian tanks.

I was wearing ski boots, but the snow filtered inside, freezing my feet. Yet, because of my fur-lined coat, I probably kept warmer than any of my companions. As our journey continued, that cozy coat became a house, bed, a blanket and pillow. That was the best decision I made when choosing necessities to take. I thought the photographs were the most important of family treasures, and I had already lost them! It was my fault. I unwittingly left them on the counter at the office in Lüben.

By 11 a.m., when we arrived at the little town of Haynau, the only foot without frostbite in our group was the wooden one.

At Haynau, we registered with the authorities to get a ration card. They assigned us to a home owned by a family willing to put up refugees. The two daughters of the Teicherts family gave up their room for Eva and me. The mother fed us soup before we fell into bed, and then we slept all day and the next night, waking only from fearsome nightmares. The next morning, the lady of the house gave us breakfast before we started out again.

As we traveled, scores of other refugees crowded the road ahead and behind us. Our hearts went out to them, as we were in our prime and healthy. Most of those around us were elderly or mothers with babies and young children. Even the ones in wagons were not unsusceptible to frostbite. Sitting still in freezing weather could be worse than walking. Animals suffered, too. We watched sorrowfully as a donkey struggled to pull a farm wagon loaded with children and belongings and yet missing a wheel.

I later heard of a baby so ill that his relatives were ready to throw him off their wagon. His mother had to eat to nurse him, but there was no food. His grandmother insisted on cuddling him and gave him water. He survived to become a successful businessman.

Along the way, we passed through Bunzlau and then trudged on and on. As we entered Görlitz at 4 a.m. January 28th, I remembered that a boarding school chum, Archangela Melcher, was from there and lived on Blumenstrasse. We found the house, but "Arche" was not there.

Even at that hour, her gracious mom took us in. After we had slept, she let us scrub ourselves and wash our clothes. Never having seen a washboard, I rubbed my knuckles raw trying to get my ski pants clean. We spent one more night before taking off.

On February 6th, the four of us finally reunited with our Hitler Youth group at the Wigandsthal railway station. They were watching for us. We and they were relieved to find each other. Someone snapped a photograph there. At that moment, they were our family. Wolfgang, whose wife was in Hessen with her parents, said that he had gotten orders to take us to Spindelmühle in Sudetenland. That is where the Germans had a sanatorium/rest and relaxation site for weary servicemen (mainly Navy men from submarines, known as U-boats), who needed a brief getaway.

ABOVE: Hitler Youth staff members begin their trudge from Lüben to Haynau, after Hanna's foursome departed. January 27, 1945. BELOW: They continue their march through Bunzlau. Late January, 1945.

But for then, we would rest in Wigandsthal. A castle there was occupied by a large group of German girls, who had been learning to be housekeepers. As I wrote in my pocket journal, "They marched out; we marched in."

After the evening meal, as we snuggled in our warm beds, refugees banged on the doors on and off all night, begging to come in from the snow.

All the time we were there, the knocking and pleading continued, night and day. I hope it was not our Lagerführer who made the decision not to let them in. Surely, the person in charge of the quarters assumed that cruel authority.

On February 12th, my friend Eva took off for Melsungen in Hessen, to stay with her sister-in-law. I would surely miss her.

Five days later, we left the castle and began walking, riding a train, walking again in the direction of Spindelmühle. Passing through Neustadt, we moved on to Friedland, where we spent the night, and then on to Bad Oppersdorf and, passing through Zittau, to Hainewalde, scene of an awesome mountain, a wall of ragged stone.

Our leader tried to get us on a train going south, but all were headed west. Thus, we had to walk another half day to a railroad station to catch one that would take us through a mountain pass to Spindelmühle. That ride extended on and on, not because of the great distance but as a result of constantly having to stop for safety. We prayed that bombers would not unload on a sitting duck. In the middle of nowhere, we were delayed for 24 hours because of "obstacles and bombing," according to my journal, which added, "We had nothing to eat or drink."

At Rundstal, the plan was to change to another railroad. A special train was supposed to depart at seven o'clock in the morning. Nine hours later, it still had not left the station. When we finally got on, it took another night and day to get to Alpacca.

Despite all these hassles, we were a fortunate group with priority. Many refugees were directed into coaches headed to certain cities, with no say-so as to where they wished to go. The authorities, apparently were trying to scatter the masses, not overcrowd one city or another.

ABOVE: Hitler Youth and trainers marching through Friedland. February 17, 1945. BELOW: Morning muster. Hainewalde. February, 19, 1945.

ABOVE: Hitler Youth with some staff members waiting in the slush of a train station. BELOW: Another wait at another station. En route to Spindelmühle. February, 1945.

ABOVE: All aboard—onto a coach. BELOW: Hanna washing her hair with locomotive water. Another staff member holds up a mirror. En route to Spindelmühle. February, 1945.

Even so, all passenger coaches were dirty and crowded with disorderly (but grateful) riders—except our regimented Hitler Youth.

On the afternoon of February 28th, we finally made it to Hohenelbe.

Once we were off the train, we took a bus part of the way and then had to climb northward up a mountain to get to the sanatorium at Spindelmühle. Exhausted, we nevertheless marched up and up to our destination. At least, we were young and what awaited us was a delightful surprise.

That sanatorium was a resort with elegant Persian rugs and leather chairs, a piano, movie projector and screen, and a staff waiting to cater to us! Our rooms even had running water. From chaos and depression, we had climbed into Heaven!

None of the sailors were there, possibly because so many U-boats had been sunk in the Baltic Sea or because the war was nearly over. We were allowed to occupy one of the buildings and were welcomed like paying guests.

This place was much more elegant than the Göhrener Hof! Maids cheerfully changed our beds every day and asked what temperature we preferred our bath water. Cooks and waiters prepared and served our meals. Not soup, but normal food, possibly supplies intended for military personnel but perhaps from local farmers, who seemed untouched by violence.

Some of our group stayed just down the hill in a bed-and-breakfast, as the facility could not accommodate everyone.

I even took a side trip from our haven back to our dear old Habelschwerdt.

From the train window, I saw a group of 15 or 20 disheveled Eastern European women in babushkas fixing a road that crossed the track. Most likely they were from a concentration camp, as a German soldier with a rifle on his back was the overseer. Along that road was a wooden fence, where one of the workers, pants down, was relieving herself.

From March 22nd to 26th, I visited friends and played with Kiki's fox terrier, Putzi, whom I had left when we moved.

Back at the resort, the boys and I took ski lessons and skied every day, as though we had not a care in the world.

ABOVE: Spindelmühle, sanatorium or resort? BELOW: Bed-and-breakfast quarters for the additional Hitler Youth. Spindelmühle. 1945.

We *did* have cares, though. No one knew for sure whether their family members were dead or alive. News from the front was sketchy. What we did hear was devastating. The siege of Breslau continued day after day, buildings on top of buildings, bodies on bodies. *Was my father among them? What about all those beyond the city limits— my beloved Omi, Opa, Kiki and the others? Had the Russians found them? Raped them? Tortured them? Worse?*

And then there were our own unspoken fears amidst all that luxury. *Is tomorrow our last day?* That was especially traumatic for our campers, but they bonded like soldiers.

Fine dining at Spindelmühle. March, 1945.

There *was* something disturbing at Spindelmühle. Many a morning, looking out my window, I could see Russian POWs walking—some limping—near our building en route to wherever they would be doing forced labor that day. While their German soldier guards watched, those bedraggled men began digging into garbage cans, fighting and beating each other for remnants of our meals. *My God, we are living so well, and they are fighting for food!*

I was aware that even Silesians and other civilians who had fled from bombs in the west were hungry. We were, in contrast, on a private oasis—but only temporarily.

When I heard that a German Army plane would be leaving for Breslau soon, I wrote a heartbreaking letter of goodbye to my father. All night, I poured out my heart, assuming we were near the end of our lives.

I could only hope and plead to the Lord that he would still be alive to read it and see the photograph I tucked into that envelope.

Hitler Youth and some staff members ready for ski fun. Hanna
is 2nd from the left. Spindelmühle. March, 1945.

Then on May 1st, came the unexpected, unimaginable
news: Adolf Hitler, our hero, our leader, was dead! Nazi radio
reports originally said he had perished "fighting the Bolsheviks
in Berlin." Later, we heard the even more shocking news that
he had committed suicide—in his bunker with Eva Braun!

Hitler's death meant that the Red Army would surely
come. I must get to Vienna. Why Vienna? We knew the
Americans were there and hoped they would feed us and treat
us like human beings.

Everyone was on their own, but a group of us started
out together on May 7th.

Our Lagerführer called me aside. Wolfgang no longer
displayed the demeanor of a military officer nor a mere co-
worker. This man had become an older friend, one who cared
about my well-being. "Hanna, I have a capsule for each of us,
in case we find ourselves in a situation worse than death."

"Capsule?"

"Cyanide. Suicide. I'll keep it for you."

I was grateful. Nothing would have been worse than being raped or tortured.

We took bicycles from the resort and decided to travel by way of Hohenelbe. I positioned my suitcase in the baggage rack on the back, hung my knapsack over my shoulder and took off down the mountain. How I managed with that heavy suitcase, nearly three feet long, balanced on my bike, I cannot imagine, but I was young then.

We bicycled for four or five hours along a road jammed with people trudging all around us. Not only was it exhausting, but it was almost impossible not to bump into fellow travelers. I lost Wolfgang. Surely, our paths would cross again soon.

Our route went through Thannwald, where, to my great fortune, we encountered a convoy of German trucks transporting supplies. I yelled to the driver of one hauling oil barrels, "Can I come up?"

He nodded.

Casting down the bike on the side of the road, I climbed atop the barrels, suitcase and all.

Now I was not the only displaced person who had hitched a ride on that truck. A mother with two children, a couple of older people and others were hopping on and off, as we rolled along.

Legions of German Army trucks traveled the same paved road with desperate refugees clinging to the sides and tops.

I hung on for a whole day, hoping no one would shoot at an oil barrel.

The truck was to go by Gablonz, but the driver went the wrong way, having been distracted by the Czechs who suddenly could not speak German.

About 30 kilometers before we reached Prague, the German trucks were halted by Czech civilian patrols with guns and arm bands of their flag's blue, white and red.

Our servicemen were herded away, we knew not where. We were also unaware that, in anticipation of the arrival of American and Russian troops, Czech patriots had been driving the Germans out of the region, and, on May 5th, had declared Prague liberated.

The next day, May 8th, became the momentous occasion that the Allies call Victory Over Europe (V-E) Day. My journal referred to it as the "Big Panic."

Everything and everyone was stopped. We were led to a camp where we had to show our papers and be searched for weapons and ammunition.

Every German civilian had to find something white to tie on one arm to show capitulation. Someone gave me bandage fabric, and I stood with others terrified. It got worse!

Word spread quickly as we took off walking. "The Russians are here!" We saw them robbing passersby—Czechs, too!

A crowd of us took off. None ran. We did not want to call attention to ourselves. No one knew where we were headed, we just kept going and praying. Women with children and belongings in baby carriages or carts, old people with sacks on their backs—a motley assembly of humanity. Local soldiers motioned to us to move along, pretending they couldn't speak German. They were afraid, too, as Sudetenland had suddenly become part of Czechoslovakia.

At Theresienstadt, American GIs were helping the Russians control the Germans. It was the Americans who liberated a concentration camp just as we were walking by. Bedraggled former prisoners—women—attacked us with great fury. They were yelling "G.D. German pigs!" and anything else ugly they could think of. Two grabbed me, pulled the combs out of my hair and stripped off my leather riding jacket, a gift from my aunt in America. Still clawing at me, they jerked at the rest of my clothes, but I ran like the devil, and they turned to attack someone else. My fine wool scarf had been stuck in the sleeve of the jacket they stole, but the loss of that was nothing compared to the near loss of my blood.

After the scare of my life, crowds of us with white arm bands were herded to walk on and on, depressed, with only a glimmer of hope that we could reach an area occupied by Americans, before we got whisked away in cattle cars—or worse. A German girl, I knew, could be a "prize" of war.

We became only a small part of the four million Germans fleeing westward to the British or American Zone, but our numbers increased every kilometer. So did the chaos.

At one point, I literally trampled on money. German military paymasters had bundles of cash and feared they would get caught with it. They flung it into the air. Tempted, we were afraid to take it and walked on it. Passersby were saying "It's no good." "Not worth anything!" "Those Marks are like Pfennige (pennies)."

When we reached Leitmeritz, two or three of us girls were hosted by a nice German family, who let us spend the night.

My May 11th journal entry reported that we had been through Lobositz, Aussig and Türmitz and to a small village, where we were able to stay overnight in a barn.

In one of those towns, some of us were allowed to stay in a home, guarded by turncoat Czechs. We found out the next morning, that, while we were sleeping on the kitchen floor, Russians had come banging on the door. Our guards insisted that the house was empty and encouraged them to leave. I never heard a sound! Even more astounding was the fact that the homeowner's wife and children had been hiding in the fields, afraid of what the occupying forces would do to them.

Masses of people jammed the roads with us, most of them moving west. But at one place on a Czechoslovakian road, we encountered refugees organized in a group, singing "Silesia! Let's go back to Silesia!" They tried to persuade me to return with them, but I wanted to go to America and moved westward.

Often, when we entered a town, we would stop at a railroad station, where others like us gathered. At one, I was so exhausted, I placed my coat next to the outside wall, tumbled on top and fell asleep. Not the rumble nor a whistle or chugging of trains coming or going woke me up.

Somewhere on our route, a POW camp apparently had just been opened, and American soldiers were milling around inside and outside the gate, some talking with citizens, others avoiding them. They looked better fed than anyone around them. Tin food cans littered the road near the fence.

We picked up a few from ditches that some of those guys had not finished. Despite the flies and no fork, we ate hungrily from the cans. I wondered later if that had been a game, to see if we refugees were too hungry to be proud.

At another town, trains were going east loaded with Russians. Some called to me and other girls, enticing us to go with them. They asked for water. We had none, so they cursed at us. If I had had a cup, which one would I have given it to? I shook with fear and distrust. They were all thirsty. The others would have cursed me, spit on me or banged me on the head.

I was a teenager, 19 years old. Everyone knew what Russian men ("barbarians" to us) did to girls in countries they conquered. No female with common sense would accept their entreaties. "I'm going west," I said confidently.

Poles wanted revenge. We German girls knew not to trust them either. Thus we stuck together with other Germans of all ages, and we prayed a lot day and night all along the trek.

At that same depot, a Russian soldier came up to me to say that one of his officers wanted to sleep with me. I thought that unusual, because most went on a rampage, taking whatever they wanted. Even so, I anxiously expressed a definite "No!" and moved quickly away.

Still scared, I asked a railroad signalman who was moving tracks if I could hide in the station.

"No, no! Get out of here." He was afraid, too.

I ran back into the depot anyway.

Another time, occupying Russians were milling all around, eyeing young girls. As we were passing a tall rock formation, several of us decided to use a deep crevice in the stone as a hiding place. There was talk that the Americans were coming. Perhaps we could wait for them. Bad idea. We could neither lie down nor gather food. Besides, we feared being left behind, and barbarians would have us trapped.

All of us jumped back into the road and moved along with the next group passing. Fright permeated everything, even our judgment. I threw away my ID, because I did not want a Russian to know I was a German citizen.

Farther along, I was still on my own, but I had hooked up with other girls, women and children. Two of those girls became my friends. Mia Gronemann, who was from a town near Kassel, was probably 25. Otti Miersen, from Hamburg, may have reached her 21st birthday. They were opposites. Plain but nice, Mia may have served in the military, but in ragged civilian clothes, she faded into the crowd. Otti looked like a starlet with plucked eyebrows and black hair. She appeared amazingly chic, even in old ski pants. Despite our differences, we needed each other.

We encountered three Russian soldiers who, according to scuttlebutt, had been on a three-day drinking and raping spree. They dragged a pretty pregnant woman over to the side of the road to rape her. We could hear her scream and fight back, but no one was brave enough to rescue her. We would have been shot.

It was just a matter of time before that would happen to me, I knew. They could spot me as a German with my red hair, dust from head to foot and a white arm band. If I had had my designated pill from Wolfgang, I would not be here today. I hurried on.

I know that there were many lost children along the way, many rapes, and deaths from frostbite in the winter, heat exhaustion in the summer, starvation and old age. Others have told about corpses beside the road, but I never saw them. For awhile, I felt as though I were a *walking corpse.*

How fast did I walk? At times, up to approximately 55 kilometers a day. That is a little more than 34 miles.

Our impression of the conquerors varied from "They're nutty!" to "Those drunken bums!" to "How dumb!"

For instance, we observed some guys from the Red Army riding bicycles round and round like little children, little *drunk* children. Quite a few of those were slanty-eyed Mongols. Others were screeching on accordions without a clue how to play them.

In one area, they were taking everyone's watches. We guessed the Soviets had never seen watches before, because none seemed to know how to wind them. When a fine gold one would stop tick-tock-ticking, they would trade it for a little silver one that was still wound. Then there were the collectors, who wore multiple watches all the way up their left arms.

I also heard that those guys had no idea what to do with a toilet. The word was that they washed their feet or their potatoes in them.

If we were lucky, we might find a barn or shed, where we could hide and sleep. Several girls my age were sleeping in haystacks one night, when some Russians barged in with pitchforks and began poking the hay looking for a female "prize." I didn't notice. I was too sound asleep. Some of our walking companions told me in the morning.

Our legs were tired so we climbed into a freight train and arrived in Seestadel, where we stayed 24 hours still in the train. Nearby, occupying forces had found weapons and ammunition and, thus, were marching a military surgeon and 21 soldiers across a field and into some woods to be shot. Other occupiers threw us off the freight car. "The situation became critical," I wrote.

Moving along from there, we did not have a pass identifying that we were from Czechoslovakia, so we had to get out of the next village.

As we treked on and on, German soldiers had joined us. We females felt less vulnerable with them nearby. But Russian troops noticed them, sorted them out and marched their enemies inside wire fencing in the town of Görkau.

Some of us cried, "We want to see our husbands!" in pitiful, begging tones. Crazily, we thought we would be safer inside that fence. Each of us picked out a face we had seen in the crowd and pretended he was our beloved. The guys went along with it, but the Russians only let us say "goodbye" and ordered us out. "Go home!"

We tried once more to get into the camp, but we did not have an ID, and, again, they turned us away. We hung around another night.

While seeking a place to hide, we came upon a Dutchman and a Pole. The cold-hearted Pole domineered the Dutch guy. Both had been workers in Germany. The Dutchman was really pleasant; the Pole, a bull, who wanted one of us girls to do you-know-what. We told him you-know-what.

The next day, we marched onto Komatau, where we met Kurt Hartwig, a German who was with a Frenchman and a civilian Czech guard. They let us go by, pretending we were Dutch.

Hunger encouraged us to do the unthinkable. Passing by a field, we saw rhubarbs just right for the picking. We picked—and ate! At home, we would have enjoyed them cooked with sugar and a bit of lemon peel in a delicious torte. Stepping off the road, we pulled them up, wiped them on our ski pants and wolfed them down. Ooowee! Sooour! You've really got to be hungry to do that. We were.

As Mia, Otti and I moved along together, not one of us spoke of our past, former jobs, boyfriends, aspirations or even close family members. Our concerns surfaced moment to moment.

Mia, who trudged head down was more likely to warn us of obstructions. "Watch out for that bloody boulder!"

Spotting a healthy Germanic male headed west on the road, Otti would nudge us to his side and strike up a conversation. "You going to the German border?" She continued a banter, allowing him to be our guard until we had to stop to rest.

As the friendly but more tacit one, I stayed on the lookout for food sources and appropriate city halls giving out food rations and accommodations.

Occasionally, we noticed that people of that region who had been Germans became Czechs overnight. We never saw any local women. Then we met a German serviceman named Hofman, an escapee from that camp back at Görkau. He replaced some of our newly-made female friends, who had scattered to other destinations.

"Now we are worried," I wrote in my journal. "Should we go to Chemnitz by train? Or is the Army (American)... someplace else?" Then when we reached Chemnitz, I quickly scribbled, "There are so, so many foreigners here. I'm afraid to speak German...they might make us sweep the streets like the others."

The four of us grabbed (literally) the first coach back to the last station, standing on the doorway steps, clinging to a handrail.

More walking took us to Braunsdorf, where they put up refugees in an old hotel. We slept on the floor, but this was a place where we could get food served from their kitchen. They even baked cakes for us! At one meal, they apologized that the only meat available was pork from diseased pigs. We were so hungry, we ate it anyway and never got sick.

No longer fearful, we decided to stay for a few days to rest and observe the situation. Hotel Flecksig housed many travelers who could give us advice. The rumor was that the Americans were near there. We did not know where.

So, during the daytime, the three of us snooped around to try to find them. Much of that time, we spent in a large wooded area so as not to be seen while spying.

Back at the hotel, we heard that, on May 24th, 600 people would be transported to the west. To apply, we had to go to Frankenberg's mayor. "That is bad luck," I wrote. *Why should we travel such a very long distance just on hope?*

It began to be obvious that the GIs we sought were in Saxony on the other side of a canal.

On May 21st, a new buddy, Willi, went spying to check out the possibilities of our getting there without any Russian interference.

With Willi to guide us on May 22nd, we skeptically considered a bombed-out bridge, only about 100 feet long, as the best route. No vehicles could cross it, but Mia, Otti and I tried to balance ourselves along broken pieces to get to the other side, determined not to look down—*way down*—at the water.

We made it. Willi, too.

Our next stop was Lichtenwald, where, for some reason, we thought about going back to Chemnitz, also in Saxony.

The first American we saw was a guy sitting on a chair at a checkpoint, his helmet in his lap, rifle against the wall— sound asleep! At first, we did not dare try to go by. Someone could have killed him! At least, he was not likely to attack us. Needless to say, he left us alone. We kept walking. "This made a good impression," I wrote.

My journal notation after that was: "At the moment, we are sitting at a railroad station in Cossen. Willi is looking for night quarters. We heard that the Americans are very friendly toward people here. Let's see if it will happen."

Once our threesome entered into what we assumed to be the American Zone, we had a completely different attitude about ourselves and our future. We could see and feel the difference.

The men in uniform there didn't seem very dangerous. We watched them hand out candy, gum and toiletries like shampoo and toothpaste to children. Kids would be hopping all around them. A few GIs even shared some K-rations with us.

As a convoy of Army trucks with white stars on them passed, I saw the first black faces I had ever seen outside a circus. Two smiled at me, but I was too scared to smile back.

Other trucks with white faces yelling something at us rolled by. Yes, I had learned English in school but could not understand them. Maybe that was good.

The German states Saxony and Thüringen, we later learned, were in the Russian Zone but at that time were occupied by Americans, so we felt relatively safe.

We encountered no problems in Cossen but had a horrible night in a half-open barn farther down the road. Nowhere was there anything to eat. For the first time since we crossed into Saxony, our attitude changed again. We were feeling sad, even losing our incentive to go on. I had to tell myself, *No! We have today!*

Later, we heard about a train leaving Altenburg. We had to go through Ober-Gröfenhain, where it rained really hard. My two girlfriends and I found cover in a restaurant. Such a deluge of rain seemed to be against us, but we plodded on to Jahnshain, where we finally found "wonderful quarters."

On our trek to Altenburg, we saw in the woods, under strong American guard, prisoners, who were from the German Army. "This," I wrote, "leaves a terrible impression. I feel so sorry for them." Then I wondered, "Who knows what's going to wait for us?"

A bit farther, we overheard voices in a wooded area and saw a number of burnt German planes.

Caught in the swerving lava of faces and feet, we heard and spoke such comments as: "My feet are sore—I've got to stop." "Hear that poor baby cry—he must be *so* hungry." "Wonder where we can sleep tonight." "Oh gosh, if it would only stop raining." "Is that a Russian over there? Let's get out of here!"

In Altenburg, we were able to get a pass to ride a train to Zeitz. There, after a long search, we found a nice place to stay. The next morning, we seized the opportunity to ride on a coal truck to Theissen.

"Now we...hope that we can hop on a coal train that presumably will be under American watch. That would be a loss, if we have no luck." As I wrote that, I knew the risk we might be taking.

We did it! We found another means of transportation besides our worn out feet: a coal brickette train. A red caboose, to be more exact. That crew's car was too full for one more human being, but the three of us girls and one German soldier crammed into the tiny look-out compartment on the roof intended for one man. It was terribly cold up there. We huddled together while the engineer moved us slowly, stopping repeatedly but nevertheless getting us to our destination faster than our tired legs could have taken us.

The soldier who had joined us was Klaus Schrage from Olpe. I asked him if he knew my famliy's friend from there, Mrs. Brinck.

"Oh, yes! A wonderful lady!" He enthusiastically shared memories with me about a woman I would love to see again.

The next night, we were sitting in the half-open room of a totally bombed-out railway station. At five o'clock in the morning, a good-natured station master woke us up to say that we could take a V-1 train. Among the most deadly of German weapons was the V-1 flying bomb and the improved version, a V-2 guided rocket that destroyed cities of Great Britain and terrified its inhabitants. This train on its way to France carried one rocket per flat car. Once again, we climbed up into the look-out compartment, ready to ride. But an American soldier told us "in the nicest way" that we had to get out.

Our feet were inflamed and crusty with sores. When no one was looking, we stepped up and slid onto a platform next to a rocket. But that didn't work either. He chased us away.

A coal train rolled by a little later. We decided to wait for something better. Nothing came, so we took off on foot.

After Gotha, we arrived in a small town where a nice druggist, who was from Breslau, gave us toothbrushes.

My next entry, dated the 27th of May, told of a guy in

the Eisenach railroad station allowing us to sleep in a store attic with hay on the floor.

Later, we had to wait for tracks to be moved. Then, after we climbed up on a freight train, two of the American occupation forces made us get down. It was not possible to go from Thüringen to Hessen, we learned, without a pass. Actually, we had one, but it did not have the American stamp for Eisenach. Thus, we spent another night in that town.

In the morning, we started walking across a field, the autobahn and into a forest, trying to avoid a Belgian guard checking for passes.

Farther along, we passed an American guard, who said nothing to us. This was Hessen, definitely in the American Zone! Our spirits soared.

At Braunhausen, we got fantastic quarters with good food. Otti, Mia and I, at that point, vowed to go to Gutenburg. But then we thought of Melsungen, where my friend Eva was, as far as I knew, staying with her sister-in-law. We still did not have a pass. To get one, we must go to the commandant of Rothenburg.

The word was that he was known to be nice, but Belgian soldiers were there, too. "Those guys we want to stay away from under any circumstances," I reminded myself. According to other refugees, they were rough and unforgiving.

After a debate, we moved on to Heinebach.

The next day, we helped the Bürgermeister, Mr. Kleinschmidt in his office in return for lodging. Until then, we were seriously thinking of going to Melsungen—or perhaps to Mia's stepmother's house. I mused in my little book, "Maybe we should stay here. The people are so nice. She (our hostess) took good care of us, gave us butter, bread and two kilograms of sausage!"

We decided on Melsungen. A nice police officer offered to hold a seat for us on a milchauto (dairy delivery truck) headed in that direction. We took him up on it.

On June 1st, I wrote: "We are lying (next to) a country road and have had a wonderful breakfast. Right there, an American comes to us. He wants to smooch with Otti." I laughed myself half cuckoo.

In Melsungen, the parents of Wolfgang's wife had taken in Eva, her mother and now us. Though grateful, by our third day there, we sensed that the situation was not great.

Eva's sister-in-law had a retarded baby—and an American boyfriend! Wolfgang had not been heard from, yet neither had he been declared dead. The Russians probably got him, but maybe he found time to take the capsule.

Although the family who owned the home treated us well, we kept hearing from Eva that "they are nasty and have no heart."

We thought Eva and her mom should both get out, but Eva started working on a gentleman's farm on that Monday, so we left Melsungen as fast as we could.

A driver offered us a ride in his car. After accepting, we realized it was headed in the wrong direction. We got out fast.

I had a miserable toothache, so I quickly found a dentist, and, as soon as he finished pulling my infected tooth, we waited on the road in hopes that a car might come and take us to Kassel. Unfortunately, not. One German driver pointed at us and made a gesture that means "Are you nuts?"

That's when we started walking until two American GIs gave us a lift in an Army truck. They handed us chewing gum, chocolate and cigarettes. I enjoyed the first two, but I never smoked and did not know that we could have bartered with the cigarettes.

When they let us out, we went back to the autobahn, where we walked and hoped someone else would pick us up.

Too bad that Eva couldn't come. I did not want to stay with those people. I'd rather be free and hike.

On the third day away from Melsungen, we were staying in a refugee camp at Nielsungen, when I recorded that "We just had a lot to eat. A little beer, too." I never liked beer. That night I may have felt differently.

The authorities offered us a job cutting tobacco in the morning. Although tempted, we declined. Still without a pass to go from one state to another, my friends and I pressed on.

On the 6th of June, we came upon Landwehrhagen, a village which had suffered greatly when the Americans tried to bomb it to pieces. The three of us were allowed to stay in a camp there overnight and moved on to Hann-Münden. This was Mia's hometown, just outside of Kassel.

Of course, Mia invited us to stay in her home. A simple worker's house, it was undamaged by the war. Her father was not there, but her stepmother and step-siblings welcomed, fed us and let us share a bed.

Otti and I stayed there three days.

By then, we had nothing but ski outfits. Nothing. My socks were worn away inside of what was left of my ski boots.

Mia's stepmother, Mrs. Gronemann, gave us white fabric, and Otti made us each a skirt with straps.

The Americans had been in that region a long time, so all the cafes were open. Mia took us to one, where we savored really good coffee.

We felt very self-conscious, though, as anyone could see that we resembled a trio of gypsies.

In some towns, German citizens who were asked to put us up, looked at me haughtily and said things like "Look at you!" "Where do you come from?" "You have nothing!" They reminded me of my stepmother's disdain for my friend, a kitchen worker from the Hitler Youth camp. I wondered if people were now asking *her* such questions.

Late that same afternoon, we went to the Weera River, where we could bathe and go swimming. Some "Amis" (We called Americans "Amis"—pronounced Ahmees—and Brits "Limeys.") were hanging out near there.

On my wrist, I had a beautiful heavy bracelet my grandmother had given me. Its lock had come loose, so I had stuck in a piece of red paper to hold it tighter. Concerned that I might lose it in the water, I asked one of the four GIs, "Would you hold this for me, please?"

"Sure," he said, taking it from my hand.

When I went back to get it, he swore he had never gotten it. The other witnesses did not contradict him.

We had heard that some Americans were taken out of prison and sent to the front lines. Could these guys have been those criminal-types?

Or was our good impression of Americans completely wrong?

IV. The Flight Continues

After the three-day rest with Mia's family in Hann-Münden and a swift train ride to Kassel, Otti and I plodded along toward Hamburg in the British Zone. Her goal: to locate her family. Mine: to find a ship headed to America. I was willing to cook—do anything—on that vessel just to get to the United States. Surely my uncle, "Crazy Josef," would take me in.

Again, we were walk, walk, walking. The numbers of refugees on the road were about the same as in the Russian Zone. The difference was their destinations.

In the Russian Zone, they walked to get out; in the American and British ones, to get somewhere. Almost everywhere in both zones, local citizens tried to be helpful. In village after village, we got food and a place to sleep. If I was lucky enough to get a three-pound loaf of bread, I could eat the whole thing in one sitting. Ration cards and a permanent ID or temporary pass were essential. I could only get cards and passes.

As Hamburg was still a long way away—from middle Germany to the North Sea, Otti and I began to hitch rides on the railroad. Passenger coaches were few and far between, so we opted for freight trains. Because many tracks had been destroyed, we at times had to get off and walk to find a train beyond the bombed area.

In that part of the country, we saw more destruction than elsewhere—more flattened buildings, gutted vehicles, blackened earth. Thus, depression and hope battled inside me.

Often a locomotive whistle seemed to wail, mourning our plight. Other times, it trilled an encouraging "Let's go!"

Refugees were hanging on train sides like grapes. Once, we got on top of a freight car. As we were traveling through Westphalia, there were numerous tunnels along the route. That was scary! Although the engineer passed slowly through those dark caverns, it occurred to me that I could fall off, then be run over by another train and never be heard of again.

Another day, we found an empty freight car with sliding

doors. Most travelers rode standing up generally, except the mothers with babies, to get more per car.

In the heat of summer, body odors clashed with the putrid aromas of stomach illnesses and urine. I settled on the first step of the open sliding door, where I could dangle my sore feet, breathe fresh air and stay cool. *What if somebody pushed me off or accidently fell against me, knocking me onto the roadbed?* I didn't care. I had the best seat in the house!

Along the way, we stopped in Siegen, where we were completely weakened from the rain and took cover in a windowless building along the railroad tracks, and in Finnentrop, where we were not treated well, so we rented a room in a hotel.

On June 14th, we thought of a better alternative to Hamburg: Bochum! My German grandparents' cousins, the Skibas (Polish spelling), whom we called Lissi and Onkel Bernard, had stayed with Omi and Opa at the Kanth home during the bombing of Bochum, so I was hoping they would take me in.

Otti and I sneaked into a passenger train to get there, a practice known among the homeless as "to ride black."

That evening, Otti and I finally found Wielandstrasse 26. As soon as I saw the bombed-out apartment house, I knew my plan was unrealistic. The building had been designated Notwohnung (temporary emergency housing), unfit for human habitation unless there was no other place to go. They greeted us warmly but were obviously old, frail and terribly unhappy. Not much was left of that second-floor apartment.

"We have nothing for you," Lissi said sadly.

That was obvious. Most of the windows were out and the atmosphere reeked of misery.

These were the first family members I had seen since the advance of the Russians into Germany, the only ones I knew to be alive, so we stuck around long enough for us to appreciate the caring relationship only a relative can show. Until I came, their loneliness must have been unbearable, as they were unsure of the fate of their three sons (all German soldiers). I learned later that, just after our leaving, Erich, their middle son, came home.

On the 19th of June, we caught a truck that took us to Ahlen. Then three black GIs, who were headed in the opposite direction, offered to give us a lift on their way back. We never saw them again.

At 9 p.m. we marched along the autobahn, stopping for the night in a very scary village. Everybody had to be off the street by 10 p.m., according to the Russians and Belgians, who were on watch. Yes, we were in the British Zone, but in the early days after the war, the armies helped each other out.

After having nothing to eat all day long, we got no ration cards! I noted one more thing: "We were given one spoon of potatoes and one cup of water. POOR GERMANY!"

All we could do was wish for more luck the next day.

As we continued toward Hamburg, Amis in trucks passed us and yelled something, but they were going in the opposite direction.

We noticed that the Limeys never gave anyone a ride.

In the morning we rode in a cement truck as far as Bielefeld. There, after we split to speed up the process of finding a night's lodging, Otti reappeared with great news. "A builder gave me 50 Marks!" I rejoiced with her, never asking why that guy happened to be so generous.

The next morning, we got the advice that we could have a ride to Herford on a truck and, the following day, another ride to Hannover.

As we approached the central part of Westphalia, the region known as Germany's "coal pot," where the mines are located, the only place we could find to sleep was a bunker. It was dark and nasty. I told Otti, "I'd rather freeze to death than stink to death." I rolled up in my coat outside the opening.

Soon after that, my friend and I climbed the ladder up into an empty coal car. That is, empty of coal. Plenty of other people like us were headed toward the North Sea.

That train pulled into a loading area of a mining company, so we hopped off and caught another one leaving there going our way. That one was fully loaded with coal, so we mounted the pile and rode on top.

Imagine what we looked like when Otti and I got off. Coal dust coated our clothes. Our skin was a slimy gritty gray. Our eyes were made up with black mascara, the color of Otti's tangled hair. No matter. We had made it to Hannover!

Hannover seemed almost peaceful. While lying on the floor of the railroad station, I wrote, "People dress nicely and they can buy cake!"

From Hannover, we rode in a baggage car to Harburg. In great frustration, I penciled into my notebook, "But now we get into trouble: We are told that in order to cross the large Elbe bridge we would have to wait six days to get a pass."

That is, to walk across. Ah, ha! But an automobile could zip across without anyone showing a passenger's pass. So...a helpful driver took us directly to Hamburg's train station. "SUPER! There we get green beans for lunch."

This city had taken the worst beating of any I had seen. We knew about the destruction of Dresden and Berlin, but Hamburg, too, had been pounded by bombs, leaving fine buildings mere skeletons or charred corpses in the rubble.

Our immediate task was the search for Otti's family. I wrote: "Once we get to their street, we see that they are all bombed out. We also hear that her mother (Mrs. Miersen), another daughter and grandson are at a refugee camp in a school at Bismarckstrasse."

At the camp, we were assigned to quarters 26 to a room on three-tier bunk beds. When Otti entered our room, a woman looked up, stared and then began screaming.

Otti answered her squeals of joy, almost drowned out by more excitement from another lady and a boy of about 8. Soon, they were hugging, crying, laughing with such gusto that I knew this had to be her mother, sister and nephew. They had no home, but they now had each other.

In disbelief, her mother declared, "I thought the Czechs got you!"

I was truly happy for this family and enjoyed getting to know them. Actually, Otti must have favored her father in appearance. Her mother and she had no resemblance. Both her mom and sister, through my eyes, seemed rather nondescript.

Mrs. Mierson offered to adopt me, so that I could get Hamburg citizenship. Great! Otherwise, I would have to leave almost immediately.

She hurried downstairs to tell the authorities that her two daughters had arrived.

The next day, I looked out at the North Sea and spotted a harbor full of US Naval transport ships. *What could I possibly do for them? Why would an American Navy captain consider even a non-paying job for a non-military former-enemy female?* It was hopeless. I returned to our refugee camp and applied for a job.

While in that camp, I met some interesting people, especially an Estonian woman in her late 20s with a 10-year-old son and an elderly mother. Annelies Feldt and her family had been there awhile, having fled the Soviets, too. When the Russians took over her country, her husband had turned into a Communist and gotten a like-minded girlfriend. A political "big shot," he had no intention of leaving.

Another kindly stranger I met in Hamburg was a druggist, who saw how haggard I looked and gave me some vitamins.

However, most Hamburg citizens looked at refugees with scorn.

Everything we owned was dirty, so we were grateful when an offer came from a girls' juvenile detention home to do our laundry for free. Among other things, I sent my ski pants and a sweater my mother had made that I had refashioned by cutting the sleeves short. Well, I got my outer garments back reasonably clean, but my bra was missing!

They had no donated clothing for women my age, but somehow I got a quarter of a Nazi flag, a pillowcase (beige from sweat and dirt) and some yarn. The only garments I had ever made were baby shirts when I was a BDM, so my sewing skills were not great. But after removing the swastika, I used the remaining red flag fabric to make a nice full skirt, which I wore with a puffed-sleeved beige (yuck) blouse.

Hamburg was a city known for its prostitutes for the sailors. Otti and I were afraid to wear our skirts anywhere near the waterfront. We had no intention of flirting with trouble, but we were curious and visited that area known as Reeperbahn anyway, just to see what was going on.

Those working girls showed their hatred for anyone whom they considered competition, an attitude we tried to ignore. Otti's beauty may have shown through her shabbiness, but they certainly could have no worries about me.

At the employment office, we had a chance to get a job as a maid, factory worker or farm laborer. Neither Otti nor I wanted any of those jobs. She hoped for one as a chemistry lab worker, but none was available. With no proper ID, I had few choices.

By July 23rd, we both began working at Paul T.G. Langbein, a crab soup factory at Stiftstrasse 15. My task was to shake crab meat in a huge sieve until only the largest pieces remained, pass it along, and reach for another heavy sieve. Otti gave up her job after only two days. Within a week, I was so tired, I felt I could not continue. Perhaps that is why I was the only woman there. Yet, if I did not work, I would have to leave the Auffangslager (refugee camp).

I contemplated in my pocket journal: "What should I do? If I don't do the right things right now, I may never make up for this. Besides, everyone is checked if they are real Hamburgers. Should I go to Bochum or to Eva (Simms) in Melsungen? Should I go back to Breslau, my hometown? Nobody can tell me that. I feel so very lonely, even though I am surrounded by so many. I am full of despair and terribly homesick like never before, that I feel I belong in a Klappsmühle (psychiatric ward). How will I continue? I don't know how this will end with me. I wake up at night with screams. I often dream of our beautiful home, and I wish that I would never wake up. If I could, I would take opium."

There was another reason I wanted to leave Hamburg.

It started with an act of kindness by a local beautician. With my extra change, I had stopped by her shop to get my hair styled. She washed and set it beautifully and then refused to take my money. Furthermore, she gave me a comb and a little pair of scissors. I hurried back to our quarters to tell of her good deed.

Because it was so hot, I had removed something I had always worn inside my clothing and placed it into my tote bag. On a leather shoelace, tied so that it hung down my leg inside my ski pants, I had carried the only family jewelry left, most special of which was my gold cross necklace from my first communion and my father's silver pocket watch from his confirmation. I added my new comb, scissors and a gift I had bought for my aunt Lissi, whom I hoped to visit in Bochum soon.

While I was working the next day, someone stole them as well as my red address book and my last 50 Reichsmarks from my tote bag.

The logical thieves were those not working. Horrified to see that my last treasures were gone, I considered going to the office and reporting the theft to our administrators. I was so shy, I delayed doing so. Meanwhile, Otti's mother and sister had rushed down there to report that I had stolen things from them, including a comb and a pair of scissors.

I would never steal anything from anybody! It broke my heart to think that my friend's relatives would do such a thing! This was the family who had offered to adopt me to help me get the identification papers I needed! I never confronted them with my suspicions. But I knew I had to get out of there.

I just wanted to be alone, and so I went to Planten und Blomen, a beautiful park, deep in thought. All of a sudden, a teenage girl came out of nowhere and slapped me hard in the face. I was so perplexed, I could not react or retaliate. Some Limeys, who had seen this, yelled, "Hit her back!"

I couldn't. She had run off, and the Limeys did not chase her. I stood there and cried and cried. I was tired of living. I have no idea how I got back to my quarters. Had I had that capsule in my pocket, I would have swallowed it.

My journal expressed my despair: "That was it!!! Whatever comes, nothing and nobody can keep me in Hamburg."

On July 27th, I was riding a streetcar to the plant when I saw a man who looked like my father knocking on a door. A lady poked her head out of an apartment window, nodded, and unlocked the door for him.

On my way home, I hopped off the streetcar on that block and raced to the building. All day, I had wondered, *Was that Papi? What was he doing in Hamburg—with that woman?*

I knocked on that same door, and the same lady acknowledged me.

"I thought I saw my father at your door this morning. He is from Breslau."

"What is his name?"

"Georg Skiebe."

With great sympathy for me, she kindly told me that the person I had seen was her brother-in-law. My hopes dashed, I also felt relief. Yet, that incident intensified the dread of hearing that none of my family had survived the fiery end of the Third Reich.

Upon arrival, I had registered with the Red Cross, listing where I resided and requesting information about my relatives' whereabouts. That humanitarian organization assisted many a refugee to reconnect with family. But now, I would be moving on, with no forwarding address.

The next day, I told my boss that I would not be coming to work any more. He was not happy about it, but he told me that I must do what I had to do. As a present, he gave me one large and two small bags of powdered crab soup.

The following day, I slept a little longer and then went to stand in line at our quarters for my soup. A woman, who appeared to be very low class, approached me. "Don't you have some other shoes?"

I looked down at my ragged ski boots. "No."

To my surprise, she invited me to her apartment, where she showed me a pair of old (20-to-30-year-old) shoes, which she gave to me before she, her husband and two kids shared bean soup with me.

I was appreciative until the head of household, the woman, shouted at me, "It's all your parents' fault that you're so miserable!" She proudly proclaimed that they were Communists, as most of Hamburg was at that time.

That woman gave me the creeps, reminding me of those females shouting from windows in that Communist neighborhood near ours in Breslau. I grabbed the shoes and got out of there as fast as I could.

All I really wanted was comradeship. I felt unhappier and shabbier by the day. *I have to get out of this city!*

On August 5th, Otti walked me to the railroad station. The only transportation to Bochum was another coal train.

As the wind blew and rain splashed, I almost froze to death in the empty coal car, even rolled into my heavy coat. But this didn't matter. I was leaving Hamburg.

Once I got to Bochum, I found out I could not stay there. I could get a permit for only four weeks. Lissi and Onkel Bernard welcomed me again at their bombed-out apartment.

I thought of Klaus Schrage, the soldier with whom I had shared another coal train ride and memories of one of my favorite older acquaintances. Grasping a thread of hope, I wrote a letter to Frau Grete Brinck, the middle-aged friend of my parents and grandparents who lived in Westphalia. At that time, her home was in Olpe, but when my grandmother got to know her, she was dating her fiancé, who lived in our apartment house. After he died, she married a multi-millionaire but came back to visit Omi and my mother occasionally.

As friendly as she was elegant, Mrs. Brinck responded by return mail, "Come, please come!" and referred to me as Hannchen (another affectionate way of saying Hanna).

"Today is August 10th and Papi's birthday," I told my journal. "I don't even have a decent picture of him. So I decorated a little medallion with a wreath in his honor. Where might he be? Is he still alive? Where is Kiki and my beloved grandparents? What I would give to talk to them. Somehow I have the feeling that I have to help them, as if they were not well off. I miss my Omi and Opa and cannot imagine that they are not in their house and very poor."

Somehow I had to figure out where else I could go. I wrote a call-for-help to my older friend from the Hamburg refugee camp, Annelies Feldt, who, at that time, lived in Salzgitter.

But just as I threw that envelope into a mailbox, I got a letter from Klaus Schrage, who had been distressed to hear from Mrs. Brinck that I was still a nomad, and he was determined to help. In fact, he had found a job for me as a doctor's office assistant. Perhaps my older friend had told him about my having worked for Dr. Winkler.

I borrowed 20 Marks from Lissi and hopped on the next train to Olpe in Westphalia.

When Klaus saw me, he could not believe the way I looked. Not only was I shabbier, but I was beat, hopeless.

He had transformed from a tired soldier in a well-worn

uniform to a businessman in a shirt and tie. Nearly ten years older than I, he seemed more handsome than when we were all disheveled, his hair blonder, his eyes bluer. He had taken off from his job managing his family's local newspaper, to drive me to the Brincks' address in his cute little gray Opel. Only "big shots" drove a car that soon after the war, and with the exception of my hitchhiking on the autobahn, I had not ridden in an automobile since my father still had one.

The home built by the Brincks in Olpe reminded me of Spindelmühle, a white mansion like America's White House atop a hill overlooking the city, but that had been occupied by the British, who were using it as their local headquarters. Their next home had been a fine stucco villa, yet by the time I got to Olpe, the Brincks resided in an old brewery building of dark brick on a large piece of land at the edge of town.

When she opened the door, Mrs. Brinck welcomed me like a long-lost daughter. Such hugging and loving words! She led me up the stairs to their second-floor dwelling quite elegantly decorated with many of her treasures from their original mansion—precious antique dining room chairs, paintings by the finest artists, exquisite draperies, more grand than those in Omi and Opa's home.

Truly ironic had been the three trips Mrs. Brinck, whom I was soon calling Tante Grete, and her daughter Eva had attempted during the bombing of Olpe. Their purpose? To carry a Max Liebermann painting, a 14th century hand-carved chest and other cherished items to Kanth.

Twice, they had to leave their train and go back, because of bombings along their route. The third time, they delivered their most valued possessions for safekeeping at my grandparents' house.

Yet, compared with many other German cities, Olpe's damage was less significant.

Had Kanth been destroyed in the siege of Breslau? None of us knew.

Eva Brinck, by the time I got there, was on her own. Her brother, Helmuth, however, still lived at home, although he was eight years older than I. Helmuth's sad eyes and a listless body were not war-related but more likely from an illness. I never asked questions, just tried to be polite, and he returned the gesture.

Tante Grete's motherly kindness I did not expect. When she used to visit Omi in our apartment house and then come over to see my parents, Papi always disappeared as though there were something about her he did not like. That affected my perception of this lovely lady, so we had never shared a friendship.

Well-educated and sophisticated, Mr. Brinck had made his fortune in the manufacture of silk stockings. When inflation ruined profits, he lost a great deal, including what we called "The White House" and their villa, but had plenty more to support his extravagant lifestyle. That lifestyle included diamond rings, one in each of several vest pockets, to hand out to his many girlfriends.

His wife tired of his romantic forays and they separated.

Originally a Catholic, she became one of the few Lutherans in Olpe. Her reason? Her father, she discovered in adulthood, had been a priest before she was born. He had left the priesthood to marry her mother.

She seemed to have a heart for refugees, unlike many Catholic townspeople. Thoughtful Tante Grete made a point to converse with them on the street and to give clothing and food to the ones who needed it.

Protestant refugees in Olpe were treated worse than Catholics. I did not grow up like that. Those scornful Catholics turned me against the church I had been taught to love.

I was one of those recipients of her generosity that very first day. To help me prepare for my meeting with my new employer, Dr. Junker, she replaced my filthy ski pants with Eva's confirmation dress and those ugly shoes I had gotten in Hamburg with a more stylish pair of her own.

When Eva was confirmed, she had been a tall 14-year-old. At 19, and somewhat emaciated from my ordeal, I fit perfectly into that well-designed navy silk dress with the white collar.

My feet were still aching and I still felt unattractive, but that dress boosted my spirits, and I was ready when Klaus picked me up to go to Dr. Junker's office.

Grete Brinck, Hanna's surrogate mother. Olpe. 1945.

As we drove toward the office, it was apparent that this was a factory town with a community of very wealthy business owners. Logically, the majority of residents were factory workers and laborers.

Once I met Dr. Junker, I knew something was amiss. His voice was apologetic, but it nevertheless deflated my pitiful ego when he said, "I would have loved to hire you, but I have already promised the job to a friend of mine."

Klaus was livid that his friend did not come through with his offer. He dropped me at the Brincks' place and roared off in his shiny gray Opel.

Before the afternoon was over, he returned with a job offer for me to be a nanny for Dr. Mueller's children. He took me immediately to the Mueller home for an interview.

Still wearing my "new" navy dress, I felt much more comfortable with Mrs. Mueller. A rather plain woman, about 5'4" with predominant front teeth and glasses, Erika wanted the best for her children, and I wanted to be their nanny. She could not believe that a nanny could play a piano.

I was hired, starting October 15th. That would give me a break, as this was early August. Sometime before my first day, I needed to get the proper papers. That meant returning to Bochum, where relatives could vouch for me.

Although I was glad to have extra time, I could hardly wait to work for Mrs. Mueller. Tall, dark and handsome Dr. Mueller, with whom she was very much in love, was not a medical doctor, but held a degree in engineering. He and his widowed mother owned several factories in town.

On August 26th, I suddenly was no longer a teenager. Much as I longed for my own family, I enjoyed the role as Tante Grete's daughter and as "sister" to Eva, who came for weekend visits.

Years later, Eva confided that her mother never was nice to her because she, a tall blonde, looked like her father, who was definitely out of favor. From my perspective, they seemed to have a normal mother/daughter relationship. With my red hair compared to Mrs. Brinck's beautifully coiffed velvet brown, I had no resemblance to any of that family, yet she was nicer to me than to her own daughter.

My trip, I decided, would be not just to Bochum but to Salzgitter to see Annelies Feldt, then to Glückstadt near Kiel. Why Glückstadt? Some family friends from Breslau had relatives there, so that was the logical place where they would have fled. Friedel and Herbert Winkler had three daughters, Marianne, who was my age, Christa, four years younger, and Renate (nicknamed Püppi), age 10. All I could think of was: *Who knows, maybe the Winklers have contact with Papi. They might even have my Onkel Josef's address in New York.*

Herbert had traveled with my mother to America when she visited her brother, so he probably knew how to contact him. Obtaining that information would be worth the trip.

After the train ride to Bochum and running around one whole day to straighten out my paper work, I spent several more days with my relatives before leaving for an adventurous trip to Salzgitter. Changing trains became quite a challenge, as I traveled via Dortmund, Hamm, Hannover and then Braunschweig, where I was stuck until the next day.

Not wanting to sleep in a stinky bunker reported to have bedbugs, I walked the streets until 10 p.m. Overcome with homesickness and anxiety, I stayed the rest of the night in the railroad station. Thankfully, I caught a train at dawn to Salzgitter, just 40 kilometers away.

It was much too early in the morning to knock on someone's door, so I took a walk down the town's sidewalk. I stopped at the local Red Cross headquarters in an old wooden shack to check for addresses of relatives. I left three cards with my name and the Brinck address on a bulletin board there and continued down the street.

Suddenly, in front of me was a familiar face: Heinz Stehr, one of the wounded soldiers who had become a Hitler Youth leader at the Habelschwerdt camp! As elated as I was, he cheered when he saw me. I felt like doing a somersault.

Already Heinz had his own business, a chemical lab and a lovely wife. He took me to his home to introduce us and arranged for me to spend the night with some friends from Silesia, who had moved to Salzgitter.

Later, I surprised Annelies and we shared a delightful time. She took me to a play, "The Waltz Girl from Vienna," and then we had coffee made with real beans and grits pudding.

Soon after dawn, I took a train to Elmshorn but was told I had to wait until the next morning to go the last 20 kilometers to see the Winklers. Instead, I decided to walk the remaining distance. Later, I commented in my journal: "On the road to Glückstadt, I met a young lieutenant, Joachim Hochmann from East Prussia, who turned out not to be a gentleman."

Our conversation had started off cordially. He told me that he was fond of Christa Winkler and gave me the Winkler address. Then he advanced on me with confidence that no one would see us on that lonely road.

I fought him off with all the strength I could muster.

Finally, at 9:30 p.m., I got to the town and began searching for that address. Once I reached it, I found that nobody was home. I waited outside their apartment. Sperrstunde (curfew) was at 10 p.m., and just before that time, Christa and Püppi came home.

Alas! Christa told me that her mother and older sister had been in the Sauerland and added, "They are on their way to Olpe to look for you!"

I was floored! How ironic!

After the long trip, I really wanted to wait until Saturday when they were supposed to come home. Christa agreed and tried everything to make that time as pleasant as possible, entertaining me with conversation and sightseeing.

The two travelers, Mrs. Winkler and Marianne, came back on Friday evening. What a time we had after not seeing each other for so long! My parents' good old friends encircled me with hugs.

In Olpe, they had checked into the fine Kaiserhof and sought out Mrs. Brinck. She knew that I planned to stop in Glückstadt, so they rushed back.

On Monday night, according to my journal, Marianne and I met some interesting guys at the local Ratskeller (town hall restaurant).

For the next couple of weeks, I relaxed with the Winklers. We had so much to talk about, and that experience was almost as good as being with my real family. And yes, they did have Onkel Josef's address. He was living in Flushing, not in

Brooklyn, as I had thought.

On October 9th, 1945, I headed home via Elmshorn and Hamburg. Then began another saga on a coal train. What a trip! I was so cold that I just ran back and forth in that empty coal car. Other refugee riders cuddled together until we reached Osnabrück. That's where I transferred to an Eilzug (fast train) with only animals in it. I hopped into the caboose.

I climbed right into a Bremserhäusel (brake house the size of a telephone booth) to make it a little easier and more comfy. In doing that I pulled, without meaning to, the emergency brake. The train slowed and stopped in middle of nowhere.

At once, some railroad personnel came to release the brake. They hollered and screamed at me. In the beginning I did not even realize that this had something to do with me. Then the door to my secret little place had been torn open. When they saw my sleepy face, the trainmen decided to leave me alone.

After pulling into Wanne-Eickel, I got out. I must have looked like a chimney sweep. At first, I was not aware why the awaiting passengers eyed me full of amazement, but once I saw myself in the mirror I knew why.

On October 11th, at 5:35 in the morning, I caught a train to Hagen, where I would catch another to Finnentrop at 9:55 a.m. "Luck is on my side," I wrote, "I could reach Olpe at 14:00, and I hope I can take care of things, because my job as nanny for the Muellers begins October 15th."

With the appropriate papers, I could now obtain a permanent ID, so that getting a job and traveling would be easier.

As I found out the longer I lived there, the British rarely checked the papers of anyone. The few we ever saw on the street were not sociable and did not give out chewing gum or chocolates, but they left us alone. Most of the Limeys we observed were passing through town in a military vehicle.

Not far from the Brinck home, the Muellers' villa was only a block from Olpe's main street and up a long driveway. Their boys were 9, 7 and 5, the little girl not quite 3. If I could keep them clean, well-behaved, entertained and happy, everyone was satisfied. The boys had to be ready for school on time, do all their homework and practice their piano lessons. All four loved drawing and sketching, our favorite activity together.

At first, I had my own small room in their lovely home, but when Dr. Mueller's brother and his wife came in from the Eastern Zone, I had to give it up.

A month or so later when another brother, his spouse and in-laws moved there from Köln (Cologne), the children and I had to sleep on couches in the large music room.

A major event in the Mueller household was the Sunday after-church ritual, a gathering of this music-loving family. The children's uncle and aunt who lived nearby joined the rest of the relatives to play Brahms and other beloved composers' music. Each family member played more than one instrument, and their serenades became a part of me.

A disappointment, such as not getting hired by Dr. Junker, can bring on a better fortune, like my job with the Muellers. My elation was apparent in my journal: "I like it so much, I could not have found a better place."

I was so glad I had had that household training with Dr. Winkler's children in Maltsch. That reminded me of my dad's mantra, repeated over and over to Kiki and me: "Learn! Learn as much as you can. No one can take that away."

On November 26th, I get a letter postmarked Cuxhaven. It was from my father and Kiki! They had gotten my address from the Winklers in Glückstadt. Papi had traveled there in hopes that they had heard from me. In the note, he asked if I could arrange for him to come.

Graciously, the Muellers offered him a place to stay in their home on the floor occupied by Dr. Mueller's mother and another brother.

And so, on December 5th, Papi came by train to Olpe to visit me. Our reunion was terribly emotional. My journal entry that night declared my joy: "Oh dear God, what a wonderful thing to see him again!"

V. Reuniting With My Family

After our joyous moments, I implored Papi to tell me how he got away from the Russians in Breslau. He had already declared that he and Kiki were fine, but I wanted details.

Actually, he did not flee, for, as a civilian, he was not to be imprisoned. The population needed to eat, so he was required to keep the sausage factory going.

Around the time of the fall of Breslau, Kiki, our step-mother, Käthe's sister Friedel, the two babies, Omi and Opa fled to Stachu's farm, but when they heard that the Russians were headed there, they rushed to the next village, where they spent one night in the basement of a stone house. When the Russians caught up with them, the females were forced to dig potatoes and cook for the soldiers in a deserted home. Meanwhile Opa had to butcher all the animals in that area, but not one of the family were given anything but potatoes to eat.

For one or two weeks, as conscripted laborers, they had to harvest sugar beets with shovels. Then they were sent to a labor camp at the south end of Breslau.

As soon as the siege ended, Omi and Opa took off walking toward their home.

Papi shook his head and broke down. "We haven't heard from them since!" Sobbing even more, my proud father had trouble getting out his words. "We're not...sure...what hap...pened to them!"

When he was better able to talk, Papi added, "We've heard that, when the Poles took Kanth, their Bürgermeister occupied my parents' home. There are no working phones or mail system, and I couldn't get out there to snoop around. Someone said that they were servants in their own house, but we don't know for sure or for how long."

He summarized what he knew of Kiki's farm labor camp experience. One afternoon, a soldier noticed the slim 16-year-old with gorgeous legs and chased her, Kiki ran screaming. Papi hesitated to admit it, but I could hear the gratefulness in his voice. "A Russian officer saved her virginity."

Then he told me that when the laborers came in from the field the next day, all their lockers were empty. Before their departure from Breslau, Kiki had sewn all of our mother's jewelry into her ski pants. Those pants had been in her locker.

Another day, a "barbarian" was showing Kiki how to clean a fish one moment and chasing her the next. My little sister outran him and hid upstairs in some hay.

When the planting was finished in May, the laborers were shipped back to Breslau to clean up. The last thing Kiki did before leaving was to plant potatoes. Again, for workers and their babies, potatoes was their only food all those months.

Poland was repossessing Silesia and half of East Prussia with a vengeance. They confiscated homes, businesses, public buildings, everything. Germans who had not fled were put to work doing hard labor. Soon, all would be expelled.

Kiki's original job was to take up loose bricks and chip the cement off, so they could be reused to fix buildings. After a period of that back-breaking task, Kiki opted to work in the Cathedral of St. John the Baptist. Water was leaking from the ceiling into the main cathedral, so walls needed to be constructed to preserve the adjoining chapels and fine paintings within.

For the first time since their journey began, my sister felt safe. Not that Soviet thieves and rapists would not do dastardly deeds in the church. Communist atheists (Russian soldiers) had been seen chasing nuns around.

Even so, because she was inside, she at least would not be spotted on the side of a road somewhere and be targeted by a vodka-swigging assailant.

Papi did not seem to want to talk about Käthe at first, but he finally let me know that she and Friedel were not protected by any officers. Both were raped repeatedly in front of Omi and Opa and their young children. As a result, Käthe contracted a venereal disease; Friedel got pregnant. Kiki did not see the rapes, for she was hiding in a rabbit coop.

At last, Papi was reunited with his wife and daughters at what was left of their apartment. Little Trautel was walking and trying to talk. They knew they were more fortunate than most families around them, who were mourning loved ones killed or maimed in the violence of the war or resulting occupation.

"Until Stephie came..." Papi's choking tears resumed. It took him awhile to regain composure, but I could hear anger in those sobs. A crazed look filled his eyes and crinkled his nose.

Stephie? I always thought of Stephie, our former maid, as lots of fun, but when Papi was finally able to tell me what she did, my opinion changed.

Stephie, who was Polish, and her Ukranian boyfriend, appeared at the apartment to accuse Käthe of hitting her in a fit of anger. "Nazi!" Stephie had screamed.

Two Polish officers appeared at the door to arrest and haul Käthe away. Quite possibly, my stepmother *did* hit Stephie during her employ, but this was too much retribution.

Almost breathlessly, Papi told of frantically searching precincts and jails "from Pontius to Pilate," seeking his wife but hampered by the fact that he could not speak Polish. When he found where she was being held, he pestered the authorities day after day trying to get her out. Exasperated, they detained and incarcerated *him!*

He and all the other male German prisoners were forced day and night to stand facing the wall of a basement room of an old villa near the Scheitniger Park. If anyone drooped out of position or dropped to the floor, his head would be banged against the wall. The basement windows were half below and half above ground level. In the daytime, Polish women would peer through those open windows to yell anti-Nazi epithets and spit on the prisoners' faces.

Finally, after about two weeks, they released him. My father had done nothing wrong!

His obsession then became to protect his teenage daughter. Meanwhile, Trautel was in Käthe's mother's care.

As Papi continued to recount the traumas of those days, his rage returned when he thought of Stachu. "He came to ask for your mother's sewing machine and Voigtländer (camera)!"

My father was seething with that memory and repeated his exact words to our cousin. "What? You blasted Polocks have taken everything, and now you want Hella's camera and sewing machine, too!" He got that crazed look again. "No!

Never! Get out!"

Dad locked his eyes with mine. "I chased him out to the street." In great anger, he added, "When that Brandbomb fell on our house, I worked so hard to quench those fires. Now I wish I had let it burn down!"

The way he treated our relative, whom I considered a sweet Casanova, was so uncharacteristic of my father. His acquired hatred of all Poles, including Mami's family, seemed irrational. Yet, the expulsion of Germans was traumatizing him.

Shortly after that incident, 2,000 Germans were being rounded up for deportation, Papi and Kiki among them. Both had deliberately worn their oldest clothes. Kiki topped hers with an American raincoat sent to me by my aunt.

Their plan had been to meet around the corner at a gas station. From there, they were hustled to a freight train and packed 40 to a boxcar, bound, they were told, to Warsaw. For work duty rebuilding one of the most bombed cities of the war? To a concentration camp? Extermination? They and fellow Germans crammed in their car speculated. Some assumed the real destination was Siberia.

From October 5th through the 10th, they stood on that train, which stopped repeatedly to switch tracks, change direction, or allow a necessity break. Polish farm women offered eggs, bread, cheese and even water for sale at some of the stops. Papi told of trading his watch, wedding band and his blazer so they could eat.

Kiki recalled Poles raping Breslau girls, but she saw something else even more shocking. Only once a day did the Poles let their captives out of the train doors. The German citizens had to relieve themselves in plain view. One modest girl went into some nearby bushes and was immediately shot dead.

Everyone was herded back into the boxcars and their traveling prison moved on and on until their engineer surprisingly steered onto a track heading westward. Suddenly, he stopped near the Russian Zone border. "Run as fast as you can!" he shouted. "Run across the border!"

They ran at first, but, just as I had done, they walked, walked, walked, until they could find a train they could board.

As displaced persons, they went every day to another

town's Bürgermeister to get one day's ration card so they could eat. All the while, Papi was determined to protect his 16-year-old daughter from Russian soldiers.

Like me, Kiki inscribed brief notes about their journey. Hers was a tiny notebook, only two by two inches, covered in upholstery fabric, so she recorded only the basics of where they slept: "October 10th - Forst - empty hotel; 11th - Cottbus - an office; 12th - Torgau - only a half-day there but went on to Halle - railroad station; 13th & 14th - Magdeburg - hotel; 15th - Heldensleben to Eilsleben - lonely old farm (Russians visited us); 16th - Sommerschenburg then back to Eilsleben - railroad station."

By the 17th, they had reached Marienborn, where they stayed with other refugees in a barn. Russians raided their refuge and, according to Kiki's little book, "took everything that was not nailed down."

As Marienborn was a short distance from Helmstedt, the border between the Russian and British Zones was only a few miles away.

German natives had recommended that, if they really wanted to get across, they should get up before dawn and sneak over the fence at Helmstedt. Thus, in the early morning of October 18th, the minister who had been their host urged them to leave two-by-two so as not to attract attention.

Just outside of Helmstedt, my dad and sister observed that guards were stationed every 500 meters along the border.

Three times they attempted to get into the British Zone unnoticed. Then Kiki crawled on her belly through a garden to the border unseen, but, as she sat astride the fence, a Red Army soldier jumped in her way.

My dad stepped up to say, "We must cross to get a permit to come back to the Russian Zone."

In the confusion of those times and the constant lack of passes, permits and passports, that was a brilliant sudden plan which worked. The soldier allowed them to pass.

Her journal reports that they spent the night of the 19th in Braunschweig and took off in the direction of Hamburg via Hannover. In Hamburg, they spent two nights in a bunker. On the 22nd, they arrived in Cuxhaven by train, where they found a place to stay despite "complications with the authorities."

On the 25th, my father and sister took a boat back to Hamburg to get their clothes from the bunker!

The teenager's notations after that could have been written anytime anywhere: on November 4th, she played cards; November 10th, she got a permanent.

When Papi was visiting me in Olpe, he mentioned that he and Kiki had been assigned to one room in another family's apartment in Cuxhaven, not as welcomed guests. The people hated having to share their only bathroom and kitchen privileges. They were not just resentful; they were furious. But they had no choice. Government officials had ordered them to give up a room for refugees.

Papi's first job was delivering coal to customers by carrying the product in a basket on his back. It did not take long before back pain forced him to quit.

Kiki was supposed to work in a fish factory, but got sick from the smells. She soon found employment at a toy company making kaleidoscopes.

I praised God that my father had found me, but my exuberance was sobered by his demeanor. This man who loved to crack jokes, dance, sing and whistle around the house seemed too defeated, too worried to ever be his old self again. At least he and Kiki had each other.

Meanwhile, I felt truly fortunate to be in Olpe with people who cared about me. And yet, my real goal was to get to America.

Christmas, 1945 was spent with the Muellers, but the Brincks invited me for an evening of holiday foods and presents. A very religious family, the Muellers escorted us all to mass Christmas Eve and Christmas Day, then we returned for singing and goodies.

Already turned away from my own faith by the way the wealthy Catholic clique of Olpe treated their Protestant neighbors and visitors, I was further repulsed by the phony Christians who came to mass drunk from too much partying and showing off extravagantly elegant clothes where so many others were struggling just to have enough to eat. I could not believe that Catholics would do this!

A holiday family dinner at the Muellers. Note the pictures of composers on the wall behind the tree. Olpe. Christmas, 1945.

I longed for the Christmases when life was more normal in my Breslau childhood. We, too, attended mass, but more reverently. At the beginning of Advent we brought in a wreath with four candles. Each of the four Sundays, we lighted an additional candle. Closer to the Big Day, Billa, who had taken piano lessons for ten years, played carols as we stood around her to sing.

Every year, our family entertained 25 factory workers at a Christmas banquet in our home. We children had to take a nap that afternoon, so we could enjoy the party at night. After the dinner, my father would disappear and suddenly a bell would ring. "Christkindel has come!" he would gleefully announce. The door to the library would open so everyone could see gifts for Kiki and me on Papi's huge desk. The toys, games and perhaps a doll would be for us children. Then all 25 guests were handed their gifts.

Those days could never be relived. I needed to stay focused on the present—and my future.

While at the Muellers, I developed a dreadful knee pain. Assuming the left knee was dislocated, a condition I had suffered while at Habelschwerdt, I bandaged it and kept going. The pain increased until I discovered that I had an infection. It began with my cutting a toenail and some skin at the same time. Although I had been going to a doctor for my swollen feet, this seemed unrelated. The infection from my cut toe rose up my leg and settled in my knee, coloring it magenta and citron.

The physician wanted to wait until it got "ripe," so I had to do my nanny job from a bed, until he could lance it. Drawing and coloring with the children and listening to the boys practice their piano was about all I could do. Meanwhile, Mrs. Mueller was very solicitous and kind.

On July 27, 1946, I started out on a trip to Cuxhaven to be with my dad and Kiki, taking time out to visit for one day with Wolfgang's sister Eva Simms in Salzgitter. She was working in an apothecary and living with her parents.

A seaport on the North Sea at the mouth of the Elbe River, Cuxhaven had been frequently bombed during the war, but residents, by then, were resuming the fishing and ship-building industries.

My family's one-room dwelling was more stark than I had imagined. No decor—just two single beds, a table, one chair, and a small iron stove for heat and cooking.

Seeing my sister again revived so many memories of good times. She was older but quite unchanged—still quiet and sad as when our mother died. Thinner than ever, Kiki no longer owned the hand-tailored beautifully-fitted clothes she had previously worn. A donated dress hung on her small frame.

By the time we were reunited, we knew of our grand-parents' ordeal. Before they got conscripted, they walked back to their home. En route, they were confronted by soldiers, who tried to stop them. Full of anger, Opa refused, thinking that they were Germans. One grabbed his golden pocketwatch; others seized Omi's large handbag. Imagine—men in uniform swiping all of a little old lady's valuables: her bankbook, cash, jewelry, their deeds and other papers, everything she treasured!

Generally mild-mannered Opa pushed those thieves aside. "I've got to feed my chickens!" he hollered, assuming they were Germans.

The occupying Russians were dumbfounded and actually let the old folks pass.

What our grandparents found when they reached their property caused more emotional pain than their stolen treasures.

Inside the house, the fine leather furniture had been ripped up, their feather beds slashed and the feathers dumped out the windows. Every trunk had been smashed. Outside, our boxer Bonko's grave had been dug up, probably in hopes of finding gold.

Sadly, they returned to be with Kiki, Käthe and their grandchild.

Omi, Opa, Billa and little Hanna when life was tranquil.
Breslau. 1931.

Only one other time had they felt so helpless in their own home. In 1939, the Czechs supposedly had opened the floodgates of a dam upstream. Omi, Kiki and I had been picking fruits and vegetables in their garden when we heard the screeching of dying cows, horses and other livestock. Seeing a wave of water coming at us across a field, we grabbed a few more veggies before the river's overflow chased us inside. Shortly, the whole first floor, where the kitchen and laundry room was, began filling up. After we returned home, it got halfway up the windows on the inside. For a week or so, my father drove his truck to Kanth with supplies daily, but first, he had to gather old chairs, wooden boards and other scraps to build a temporary walkway/bridge to deliver the groceries to his parents.

That problem could be repaired. The dilemma six years later could not.

Poles were worse than the Russians. Stealing, destroying—yes, and raping, too—was not so much for personal pleasure or greed but revenge for Germany retaking Poland. And they had official sanction. They even stole my mother's gravestone from the Breslau cemetery to be used in the rebuilding of their capital city.

Nazi Governor Karl Hanke gave orders that the German people had to leave their property. If they chose to stay, they would lose the right of ownership.

Omi and Opa chose to go back to protect what was left of their home. But not long after that, the Polish mayor who assumed authority in Kanth claimed the house and surrounding property as his own. His wife took all the Persian rugs, the huge fancy hall mirror, silver, linen and paintings of value and shipped them to Warsaw.

My grandparents were allowed to remain in the maid's quarters, for they would become servants, more like slaves, working 17 hours a day! This 78-year-old gentleman chopped wood for the wood-burning tile stoves, tended the garden and performed other manual labor tasks. The fortunate mayor's wife designated Omi to be their cook and help with the gardening.

As there was no mail or phone service available to them,

they spent a year and a half hoping the Americans would come to make life fairer. That never happened. But everything changed when they were allowed to catch the last refugee freight train to the Dutch border, where they knew no one. They had nothing, but *nothing* left.

At Gartrop, near Holland, as in all of Germany, the locals were required to put up refugees in their homes. My grandparents now resided in one room of the tiny farmhouse of a family who resented having to give up that space and hated them for the intrusion. They did not consider themselves lucky to have a fine couple with integrity, but other homeowners throughout the country found themselves stuck with gypsies, who had come from outside Germany to take advantage of free lodging and many more unsuspecting "easy marks" to rob.

Through the Red Cross, Omi and Opa had notified us of their whereabouts. Immediately, we began exchanging letters. We rejoiced that they were alive but grieved with Papi that his elderly parents must sleep in loneliness on a bed of straw.

Papi's own circumstances were somewhat better. In March of 1946, he had been employed as a Kutscher (driver of horses for rented wagons) in Glückstadt. That lasted only a short time before he got a job driving a truck for a company in Glückstadt. Being a truck driver may have seemed demeaning to the gentleman of Breslau, but Papi was fortunate to use his driving skills for more kindly bosses. At least now he was behind the wheel of a motor vehicle, even if it wasn't a Fiat, Mercedes or a Horch. Even so, he was a broken man.

His honesty had even been questioned. On Christmas Eve, he learned that the apartment owners suspected that he and Kiki stole canned goods from the basement. Neither would ever do such a thing!

Kiki and I had plenty of time to ourselves on my visit, as Papi's job took him out of town. While Kiki was at work, I spent a cloudy day on Cuxhaven's North Sea beach. Tired from my journey, I slept until Kiki came to find me late that afternoon.

"Hannah!" she screeched. Her eyes told me something was terribly wrong. "Your skin!"

It was fire red! My eyes could barely open, they were

so swollen. "Oh, no! What shall I do?"

Burning. My skin was burning, but I hurried beside Kiki back to our one-room quarters.

What could soothe me? Kiki rushed over to their only table and picked up some fish oil used for cooking, one of the few "free" (non-rationed) food products handy. "Yeah, maybe," I said hesitantly.

Gently, she tried to smooth it on my arm.

"Ah...ouch." I futilely attempted to smear more delicately. The smelly oil seemed to soothe, yet not enough. But it was all we had.

Somehow, with Kiki's help, I peeled my one-piece bathing suit off, an excruciating task, as my skin seemed to be heating to a boil. Nude on the bed, I could not tolerate the weight of a sheet. All night, I swallowed my screams so as not to disturb our multiple neighbors.

"How about some flour?" I suggested to Kiki the next morning.

Her ash blonde hair swished as she shook her head questioningly and raised an eyebrow. "Flour?"

A brief discussion later, my young sister, now my caregiver, was mixing a flour paste and smoothing it over my oily, swollen hot pink skin, forehead to toes, front to back.

As it dried, the concoction formed a crust. Amazingly, the swelling subsided. Then the crust burst, cracked and folded, giving me the appearance of a wacky zombie. Thank God, our father was not there to see his roasted offspring.

During my Cuxhaven visit, we got word that my stepmother and Trautel had arrived in Goslar at the Russian/British Zone border after her release from jail. They had been able to get a seat on a train, because Käthe's very elderly grandmother, as well as her mother, sister and little nephew were traveling with them. The Prietsch family continued on to the Harz Mountains, where relatives lived. Friedel had gotten news from her former boss that he had a job awaiting her in that area.

My father went at once to pick them up and took his wife and daughter temporarily to the Münsterlager (camp), where he, by then, was a truck driver for the British Army. Kiki and I met them there.

Once back in the family's one-room dwelling, those accommodations seemed even tinier with two more people. At least we had gotten two bunk beds.

As with all of us, Käthe seemed relieved to be reunited, albeit in strange and austere surroundings.

Apparently she had a friend or two at the jailhouse, for Käthe never complained of her experience. She must have been terribly cold in that Polish jail during the winter, though, for she was arrested wearing an ethnic costume with short sleeves.

I left Cuxhaven with a myriad of feelings from gladness to uncertainty to resentment, yet pleased that I had a better place to live and other people who cared about me.

In the early fall, Mrs. Mueller told me that my job would come to an end on October 15th, because of the shortage of food with all the extra relatives. I was sad to have to leave them, their culture and those wonderful musical Sundays.

To my surprise, October 15th turned out to be a happy day, for I received my first letter from Onkel Josef in New York. "The joy is indescribable," I wrote in my little notebook, now frayed. My pencil was getting lighter and lighter, but I never replaced it.

Frau Winkler and Marianne from Glückstadt came to visit me after I returned to live at Mrs. Brinck's. They stayed at the Kaiserhof again, but Tante Grete helped me welcome our former fellow Breslauer (Breslau residents).

Once again, I had free time between jobs. On Tuesday, October 22nd, I went to see Billa and her family. By then, they lived on a mountain top in the Bavarian woods, near the tiny town of Tafertsried. I had to change trains several times and wrote about a mishap along the way: "Bad luck again: I am in one of the last few cars, and unbeknown to me, these wagons get unhooked and remain there until the next day. The locomotive with just a few cars keeps on going to where I wanted to go. I guess the locals knew of that, and nobody had told me. So I had to spend another night at another train station. Billa and family waited and couldn't understand what had happened. There were no telephones there yet."

Once I got to the Assmanns after an hour climbing a mountain, the joy that I finally arrived was great! Billa, Albert and their three children were so close to my heart. After all, Billa had raised me.

A former German officer, Albert had been released from a POW camp and was trying to readjust to normality. Too smart to pitch hay, he was seeking a "real job" anywhere in that part of Bavaria. After I left their home, I heard that he became the director of the Red Cross in Viechtach, a hike down the mountain and an hour's train ride away.

Meanwhile, Billa had her hands full raising three youngsters and procuring food.

As refugees, they had only two rooms in a farm house. The toilet facilities were outside. Water had to be carried up and down the stairs.

The children had to walk down the mountain to school in the village of Tafertsried, where we went to shop for the meager things available.

Much to my surprise I could buy something I had not had in a long time: white rolls purchased in Gotteszell, the largest town in the area.

The owners of the farm were very very nice and helpful. They gave us milk, eggs and even shared some pork, when they slaughtered a hog. Neighbors, who were refugees from Berlin, were also friendly, especially a well-educated widow, who made scarves and mittens for everyone. All in all, those mountain people lived a rough life but had good hearts.

The most delightful events in Bavaria were the weddings. They were like a Volksfest, and I enjoyed watching the folk dancing.

My dancing dad would have been out there in the middle of the crowd, had he been with me. My shyness and not knowing the Bavarian steps nor gestures held me back.

I stayed with the Assmans until December but was determined to surprise my grandparents in Gartrop.

On my way to them, I had to pass through Olpe, so I decided to spend time there first. When we stopped at the zone border, the Amis were checking backpacks and tote bags. In my knapsack, I carried potatoes and four loaves of bread. Luckily, I rode in a locomotive to Olpe and was overlooked by nosey— and perhaps hungry—border guards.

Surprised to see me, Tante Grete was again "much too good to me." She invited me to spend Christmas there. Of course, I also stopped by to visit with the musical Muellers.

From there I made it to Gartrop, arriving December 30, 1946. I stayed with my grandparents for five weeks in their one room. They slept on a wooden bed with straw; I, on the floor. It did not matter. We were together again.

My little notebook tells my feelings. "In this loneliness, we have so much to talk about. How can I help these wonderful people, who worked so hard all their lives to have a peaceful evening of life and have enough for their family and much more? The simple people where they have to live don't like the fact that they have to share one room with them. They have nothing themselves."

Numerous small brick houses—all just alike—for workers were provided by the owners of a large "gentleman farm." Each cottage had four rooms including a kitchen. The worker family with multiple children clearly did not like our intrusion. The inadequacy of one bed for two elderly people meant that Opa kept falling off of his side, and Omi would strain to pull him back.

Just by chance did the lady of the farm hear that my grandparents came from Silesia, her homeplace. She then made a point to provide them occasionally with some extra food. Even so, to get groceries with their ration cards, they had a long walk to a village.

At times, I stared at my dear grandparents with memories of who they had been—so refined and dignified.

Tall for her era, Omi had been about six inches more than five feet, pleasingly plump with handsomely tailored outfits of unusual fabrics and exquisite jewelry. She always coiled an extra braid of human hair just her shade of brown atop her head.

With a decorating flair, her taste for putting colors together was ahead of her years. That applied to her hand-embroidered tablecloths and to the flowers she selected for her vases. Usually, women chose a single kind of fresh blossoms in a single color each week to go in their homes. Omi loved to pick a variety from her own garden and mix them in vases,

111

much to Mami's disapproval.

In Gartrop, this frail, haggard woman with cropped white hair flat against her head was at least four inches shorter. In her used, donated dress and apron, she could, nevertheless cook up a delicious meal with practically nothing. Omi would walk in ditches to find just the right herbs to flavor her concoctions. Together, we went mushroom hunting. My grandmother knew that each good mushroom had a poisonous double, and she could tell the difference.

My immaculate Breslau grandfather had been slightly shorter than his wife, but no more! His clothes shabby, his skin wrinkled on a much-thinner body, he was my broken Opa. I *did* notice a glimpse of who he had been when I watched him help Omi cut onions for supper. First, he sharpened the knife on the backside of a pottery plate, then he precisely cut each slice of onion into pieces, every one exactly the same size.

Despite their extreme poverty, Omi gave me a present with a story behind it. After the Poles had ransacked and plundered their home but before the Mayor confiscated it, my grandparents were assessing their losses. Just outside the back door, Omi found something her adversaries had dropped: my prayer book, which she grabbed to save for me! She placed it in my hand and soon was coaxing me to go with her to a Protestant church near their community. Good Catholics were never to set foot in a Protestant service, even if the only church around was Lutheran. But by then, I was no longer a "good Catholic." And yet, I had a strange feeling that I was doing wrong. My grandfather, a lifelong Catholic, seemed content.

As I was leaving Gartrop, I contemplated that despite the traumas of war, the drastic loss of wealth and social status, the deprivation of all but the most basic supply of nourishing food, how very, very fortunate our family was! Every one of our closest relatives had survived. Most other Germans we knew had lost someone they loved in war or in the flight. or—and this could be worse—a loved one had been shipped out by freight car to Siberia, Warsaw or an unknown destination, perhaps never to be heard from again.

That was not our fate.

Praise God!

VI. Normalcy, Relatively Speaking

Returning from Gartrop to Olpe, I yearned for relationships with old and new friends.

I decided to stop in Köln (Cologne) and visit the sisters who had worked for us for many years in the sausage stores. The Freudenbergers happily shared their apartment, which was petite, cozy and well-kept. They spoiled me, as though I were their little sister.

Because of them, I heard that the Bayer pharmaceutical factory in their town was looking for painters and technical artists. I went there courageously, but I had no idea what I was supposed to do. After drawing a nice watercolor, I still didn't get the job. I left my painting there.

While in Köln, I had to have another tooth pulled that had given me a hard time.

The Freudenbergers sent a telegram to our good friends, the Wuttkes in Hamburg. Had I only known they were there, my former Hamburg experience might not have been so devastating.

Evi and Lothar Wuttke, a middle-aged couple from Kanth, urged me to come and see them. Despite the bad memories of that city, I accepted their invitation.

Reuniting in their small apartment from February 10th through the 16th, the Wuttkes, their son Roland and I had a wonderful experience recalling better times.

What a comedown from the gorgeous pink (Yes, pink!) Wuttke mansion in Kanth, which I loved to visit! I had been fascinated by their spinning wheel, piano, antique music box and modern record player, not to mention their son with wavy blonde hair, who was just my height and only six months older.

As young teenagers, Roland and I withdrew from the adults and practiced our version of jitterbugging to American records. That was even more fun when some of his friends gathered for a birthday party with dancing.

A birthday party with Roland Wuttke (front).
Hanna is on the far right. Kanth. 1941.

Even listening to American music was forbidden in Nazi Germany, so that was quite daring.

Herr Wuttke, who was in his 50s, had been in a partnership with my father (before he and Mami were married) with two other partners in an electrical wholesale business. Before the Poles took over, he had also been into coal, potatoes (wholesale) and was the owner of a restaurant/bar in Kanth. Both Lothar and Evi Wuttke were well educated but Communists, like many other Hamburg residents. Even so, I was referring to the Wuttkes as Tante and Onkel, although they were not relatives.

I also found out that a cousin in Papi's family from Pollogwitz in Silesia now lived in Hamburg, and I had a chance to see him, too. Walter Kusche had lost an arm in the war.

Walter told of the fate of his younger sister, Hertel, who

was closer to my age. Those last days of the war, Hertel had been in an all-girl program learning public speaking at the General Blücher castle in Kanth. They were not allowed to listen to the radio and had no idea that the Russians were almost at their door.

Hertel got permission to check on her aunt, our Omi. She hurried over for a two-hour visit and learned of the impending occupation. Opa was angry; Omi, resigned. They warned her of the Red Army's reputation for raping, so she rushed back to tell the other girls.

All of them chose to adhere to the rule not to leave, but Hertel took off alone for the nearby railroad station. She jumped on the bumper of a departing train heading to Breslau, where she caught another to Pollogwitz. Hertel was the last family member to see our grandparents until they got to Gartrop.

Proud of his sister's bravery to warn her classmates before bucking the system to flee, Walter told me that she had reconnected with some of the girls and learned that every one of those students had been raped in their castle "prison."

But Hertel made it to Pollogwitz when the Poles were en route. The Bürgermeister told everyone to get out. The word was to go farther into the mountains. Her mother had fallen and been injured, so her father loaded his wife and a few belongings inside a wagon pulled by farm animals. He and Hertel took off on foot next to them. As desperate people were stealing food as well as family heirlooms, he had first killed a pig, boiled some chickens and stashed them somehow beneath the wagon, where they stayed frozen until needed.

Through Walter, I met a Berliner friend, Eva Rose, a very interesting person. She was responsible for the denazification of all artists in the British Zone. As art was my hobby, this third Eva in my life and I had much in common.

With the help of the Wuttkes, I bought a train ticket with five cigarettes. Even so, Walter had to lift me with his one arm and push me through a window into the crowded coach.

When I changed trains, I had to spend one night in a bunker then another night in Köln before returning to Olpe.

There, Mrs. Brinck again treated me as her daughter.

In my journal, I noted with regret, "I cannot think of

anything I could do for her in return." Then I added, "In Olpe, I found a letter from Onkel Josef that wants to be answered at once. After all, that's where I want to go."

Again through Brinck connections, I wound up with a good job, beginning March 3, 1947, with Hans-Werner and Lore König. I saw at once, that I could learn a lot there but was pleased that Tante Grete wanted me to spend Easter with her.

Herr König, whose father had been director of the Breslau waterworks, was an engineer. Hans-Werner lost his job when his industry had been denazified. At 38, he and his wife Lore, who was ten years younger, settled in Olpe. In Westphalia he was submitting freelance estimates for rebuilding bridges and canal locks.

Later, still on his own, he designed many dams and bridges in Germany and also was part of the team who designed the Aswan Dam in Egypt.

Lore's father, brother and sister were all doctors. Now, she and I would spend much of each day concentrating on our own health: finding and preparing food for the three of us. In the afternoon, I was expected to type for Hans-Werner.

Once a millionaire, Herr Rügenberg, a father with two teenagers, who owned the villa where the Königs lived, was ordered to rent out two floors. Their quarters were on the first floor. A minister (political not religious) and his wife lived on the second, and the Königs and I inhabited the attic.

Basically, my morning job was to clean house, scrub vegetables, procure food and help Lore cook. Food was so scarce that most families tried to raise what they could to become self-sufficient. That was not easy for us, as the Rügenberg home was in a very fancy neighborhood, where crops and farm animals were not allowed. Even so, instead of being a nanny for children, I had to care for their animals.

Once we had a dozen day-old chicks. Every night I carried them up to the adjoining unfinished space next to my room and took them back down every morning to a remote part of the garden until they got bigger. Then a disease killed all but one. The Königs bought more chicks, but whenever the leftover one (whom I called Piepsel) came to eat, he would come over to greet me. Piepsel became my pet.

116

The König family with Hans-Werner and Lore's first child. Olpe. June 25, 1948.

They also bought a goat, but, because she could not be kept in the neighborhood, she had to stay on the farm where she was born. Thus, I had to walk a half-hour each way to milk her. Actually, I marched my Hitler Youth steps, which got me there faster.

Because rationing allowed us to buy only 62.5 grams (an eighth of a pound, or a half of a stick) butter per month, we had to be inventive to moisten our bread. With flour, milk, ground carrots and green onions we made a tasty "smear" to be used as a spread.

Later, the Königs obtained a piece of a garden on the edge of town. This was nothing like the garden our family owned outside of Breslau. Located on a steep hill, it bristled with rocks. The ground was so hard it took a huge pitchfork to turn over the soil. Ours had been flat, beautifully designed, with play areas, kennels and flowers. The few vegetables and berries were not really for food to survive. But in Olpe, that was the main purpose of gardening.

We went to enormous lengths to obtain anything edible. For instance, Lore and I took a train to the mountains to pick blueberries all day. Of course, we ate them fresh, but we spent much time baking them, making preserves and marmalade. Right in the Rügenberg's expansive yard, we gathered acorns, cracked them open and popped them into our mouths.

My little book noted that, on April 8th, "The long awaited package comes from America." Onkel Josef sent me shoes (a nice pair of loafers) and clothes. Kiki also got a similar gift box. How did our uncle know what to buy? In our need, any size would fit, any style was attractive.

A few days later, a second one arrived. That one contained coffee, cookies, sugar and other goodies. No one wasted

117

anything then, so I proudly made a cake with the leftover coffee grounds instead of chocolate. My heart was soon banging like crazy from the caffeine! Then I got a better idea of what to do with the other can of coffee.

I rode a train to the American Zone, got off, went to a farm house and knocked on the door. "Would you like to trade coffee for potatoes?" I bravely asked. The farmer's wife was delighted with the trade.

On the 7th of June, I took a quick trip to visit my grandparents in the worst of weather, quite miserable on the two-hour walk from the train station to their quarters. In spite of that, we had a good time. I noticed, however, that Opa was not feeling well.

On June 13th, a third package arrived from the USA. Kiki and I both got white sandals from Onkel Josef. Five days later, Kiki came for a visit and helped me with my chores. Mrs. Brinck entertained her like a family member.

Kiki wanted to stay in Olpe; she liked it so much and did not have to face the situation with Käthe. But she had to get back to her job and our dad.

From July 19th until the 21st, the Schützenfest (Shoot-fest) in Olpe brought in celebrants from miles away. For the length of the fest, they never went home but dashed around drinking, dancing and showing off their skills in box-like shooting gallery booths. In all that excitement, I met many friends and got to know new ones. As I told my journal, "It is the nicest time I have had since I am in Olpe. Many well-known people from Olpe (rich and otherwise) are having a fantastic time, and somehow they are accepting me."

It was that summer of 1947 that I began to enjoy the life of a normal young adult. I had met Gisela Freeman on a train, and she introduced me to Rolf Imhaeuser and Emil Feldmann. My friendship circle broadened from there. Our favorite meeting places were Olpe's town swimming pool and a pub/restaurant known as Tillmann's for our own "fests" with coffee cream torte and wine.

Meanwhile, I was a member of a ping pong club, a Göthe Club, where we read poetry by Germany's greatest poet, and Sauerländischer Gebirgs Verein (SGV: Sauerland Mountain

Club), which sponsored hikes every Sunday. I also joined a large mixed choir that traveled around and sang "The Messiah" at Christmas and Easter and "The Creation" on other occasions.

That summer, I visited for the first time my cousin Christl Klinkert, who had been relocated to Freudenberg from Silesia. Her story was far more horrific than Kiki's or mine.

When the Russians invaded her hometown, the women were hiding in the woods. Somehow, the soldiers discovered that pretty young girl and began to pull her along. She screamed, "Help, Ma, help!" The Red Army pillagers pointed their guns at the other women.

Then her mother said to her, "Go!"

With that, the soldiers dragged Christl to the woods, where they raped her repeatedly.

Unbeknown to her at that time, her husband was a prisoner in Russia. When he returned months later, although he was ill and malnourished and she was caring for him, the former POW vehemently rejected his wife. Why? Because she had been defiled by the enemy!

For Christl, the rapes were not as devastating as her mom's single word that sent her into a nightmare to be relived for a lifetime. How could she forget that?

Back in Olpe, a gorgeous flirt never without a boyfriend, Annelies Hahn hinted that she might marry her current beau, the son of the manufacturer of the popular 4711 Cologne. His parents were not enchanted.

Nevertheless, some rumors were flying when we friends attended a party at her home on August 7th. That night, I wrote: "A nice eve at the Hahn family's. It seems that the engagement will take place, but NO!

Annelies Hahn and her fiancé, the 4711 Cologne heir. Olpe. 1947.

119

At the end—a wild dance under a traffic light, Hmm?"

My funny, singing, dancing friend (or was it her boy-friend?) undoubtedly preferred freedom.

Despite the fun of my own freedom, my journal reflects a longing for my family, a need to be with my father.

"Now I want to surprise my parents in Cuxhaven on August 8th. Only Kiki knows about it and secretly picks me up at the railroad station. That was again some trip! In Troisdorf, our train is more than one hour late, and consequently I cannot catch my train in Köln. I have to spend the night at the railroad station. It is also too late to get in touch with my Freudenberger friends (no telephone). I arrive in Cuxhaven according to plan. The surprise was great. That visit is for my dad's birthday, August 10th."

No longer did my family of four live in one room. Instead, they had been sent to one-quarter of a barracks, located on the dunes at the edge of the North Sea, once occupied by military look-outs, artillery and defense troops of the Cuxhaven seaport. "Flak Baracken" those barracks were nicknamed, slang for "waiting for airplanes to shoot at them."

Although four families were assigned per barracks, no fabric was available to mark their "rooms." At first, they got old sheets and flags from the Red Cross. Then, they would bring in pieces of wood, which eventually were used to build flimsy walls.

We could hear every word spoken on the other side, but at least no one was spying on others. Two double-decker bunks slept the five of us, and an old wood stove doubled as heater and kitchen stove.

As windows looked out to windows of the next bar-racks, Kiki and Käthe covered theirs with whatever they could find. And they had dragged in odd chairs and a table from who-knows-where.

No cake, no candles, no confetti—just being together was celebration enough. Papi brightened as we wished him "happy birthday" and sang our old favorite songs.

Just from the last time I had seen him, he had bright-ened in other ways. His pale skin had a healthy tan; his hair, a sun-bleached lightness.

Papi and Trautel in the garden at their barracks quarters.
Cuxhaven. 1947.

At age 3, Trautel still acted out the "terrible twos." Her dark eyes reflected the "devilshness" of her mother, yet she had the cute little nose and sly smirk of her dad.

Käthe became very friendly during my two days there, a phony friendly according to my interpretation, for she knew I would soon be gone. She spent the day caring for Trautel and seeking food. It was quite a walk from the dunes into town, yet, according to Kiki, she sold ration cards for cigarettes.

Still shy and subdued, Kiki stayed out of her step-mother's way as much as possible, glad to be working and out of their quarters most of the time. My teenage sister seemed thinner than usual; her skin, whiter. But then she had always hidden from the sun. If there was a nearby tree, she would stand under it. Kiki had gorgeous legs, but no one saw them, for she spread her white socks as far up her legs as possible.

As she could get coupons for clothes and our American relatives sent a few more, her wardrobe had increased. Her pride and joy (like mine) were the stylish loafers sent by Onkel Josef.

Every two years, each of us could get a ration card from an official town headquarters for a pair of shoes. Most were from Italy. None we ever saw were of leather. Generally, they were sandals with canvas strips, sometimes red with flowers, blue or another bright color. The front of the wooden sole was divided into three horizontal pieces, so you could roll your toes. Separate heels were slightly higher than the rest of the sole. At least they did not cause a painful fungus as a donated pair did.

Trautel with Papi, Käthe and Hanna. Cuxhaven. 1948.

In the daytime, when the others were working, I took a stroll on the beach during low tide. I had walked way out in a sandy canal, when some fishermen began yelling at me. *Those jerks!* I thought.

Just then, I noticed that my footprints were filing with water. At first, I didn't look back, but when I did, I saw that the water had risen behind me. It seemed to be coming from underground all around me, too.

Then quite suddenly, the North Sea loomed between me and the coast.

A swimmer since childhood, I began frantically paddling. I was swimming, swimming, swimming to exhaustion, almost giving up. *Nooooo! I've been through so much—I can't let it all end here!* One more burst of energy, and I made it. "Those jerks" did me a favor.

Once again, I enjoyed checking up on Papi and Kiki, but gladly returned to Olpe.

Then it was my turn to have a visitor. My godmother's husband, Dr. Rübekeil, who until the war's end had been a surgeon at a hospital in Goldberg, surprised me. By then, the couple lived in Westphalia, where he could not find work as a physician. He brought greetings from his wife, but what he really wanted was some way to get a substantial amount of paper for a new business venture. I took him to see Klaus at the newspaper office.

My friend Klaus obliged and gave him boxes of paper, which Dr. Rübekeil stacked on the bed of a truck, which he had probably hired in hopes of being successful. The doctor was so appreciative that he invited me to ride with him on back of the truck to their home in a tiny village near Olpe.

During my brief visit with them, I realized that neither he nor my godmother would ever recover from the death of their only son. A Luftwaffe pilot, Walter had been killed during the war.

In November, Annelies Hahn finally got engaged to the 4711 Cologne heir.

That holiday season, the Königs and I put up a Christmas tree and enjoyed being with each other. I spent the first holiday (Christmas Day) with the Brincks. Like my employers, they had decorated their tree with candles, but beautiful ornaments and shiny tinsel were added.

That tinsel reminded me of happier holidays at home in Breslau, when Papi insisted on placing each tiny shiny strip on the tree one at a time, a meticulous three-day job. Billa helped us snap the modern electric candles onto sturdy limbs and place a handsome star on top. Then, on Christmas Eve, we added delicious candy to the decorations.

Tante Grete soon was bringing in goodies on a heavy silver platter. She, Eva, Helmuth and I had to eat with sterling silverware, as the Brincks' gold tableware had been among the treasures she and Eva had delivered to Kanth for safekeeping.

On "Little Christmas" (Three Holy Kings Day, celebrated on January 6th), I rejoiced with a much happier family, the Hahns. Many siblings, their spouses and kids gathered, and soon, the majority were sitting around in the kitchen to laugh and talk and, when needed, help with the cooking. How I missed family life!

In January, 1948, I was chosen to go to Göttingen to

pick up little Roland Bretschneider, Lore König's nephew, who was coming from the Russian Zone. Since the girl who was supposed to bring Roland came too late, I visited my cousin Kurt Pragal, a doctor in Göttingen. Then because Roland and I had missed the train, he offered us lodging in his very small apartment, where I slept fitfully on a small sofa.

Possibly because I knew that Kurt's twin brother, Erich Pragal lived there, on January 24th, I traveled to Nürnberg (Nuremberg).

Far more bold than before, I proclaimed my supposed purpose: to find someone there willing to trade a sack of potatoes for my pound of coffee. That was easy, and I had a comfortable place to stay while exploring another city.

In fact, Erich's quarters were almost elegant—one huge room, Bavarian style, with three small decorative windows and attractive furniture. I slept in the bed; he, on the sofa.

Kurt Pragal

About 46 years old, my tall twin cousins were probably homosexuals, but no one spoke that word then. Both seemed successful in their very different endeavors.

After attending a culinary arts school, Erich became a chef on ocean-going ships, then worked as the head chef at a hotel in Biskra, Algiers.

He was best known for being in charge of our Führer's Gästehaus (guest house) in Berchtesgaden, where he served Hitler himself, Eva Braun and many foreign dignitaries who visited.

With all that culinary experience, Erich had become an administrator in the postal department of Nürnberg.

Another fascinating city, more interesting people! With more than 400,000 residents and no telling how many refugees, Nürnberg, the second largest city in Bavaria, was, at that time,

124

famous for its Gothic churches and buildings, a town hall with murals by the 16th Century painter and engraver, Albrecht Dürer, a museum and castle.

As I explored on my own, I linked with strangers for new experiences.

On February 1st, my journal reports "a strange meeting with an artist at the Nürnberg railroad station." She and I attended an operetta at a nearby theater.

Because of Mrs. Wieber, Erich's landlady, who "had connections," I got a ticket to one of the Nürnberg Nazi war crime trials.

Some of the Schutzstaffel (SS "black shirts") officers were being interrogated that day.

In general, I thought this was terrible. Now, I know that, along with most the of German population, I had been brainwashed, but I seriously questioned whether what the Allies had been saying was really the truth. Surely, they had made it all up.

Adolf Hitler, Joachim von Ribbentrop, Hermann Göring, and Dr. Joseph Goebbels were our leaders. We trusted them. Germany was going to win, and the world would be a better place.

All of our leaders were known as spendthrifts. People joked that the autobahn was built for Göring's little girl to learn to walk. Nothing was too good for him or his family. His daughter's pets were the most adorable lion cubs! When I saw a photo of them, I wanted one, too.

Goebbels, often pictured in newspapers, held my fascination. Our propaganda minister once studied to be a priest. He met and married a gorgeous wife, who bore him beautiful children, all blonde with dark eyes. In contrast, he was short, rather plain and walked with a limp.

Like Hitler, Goebbels avoided any war trials, for he committed suicide, along with his wife and children. What a shock! A foretelling of what was to come.

But what we had heard about the concentration camps seemed unbelievable. Who did that? Shouldn't we have known something? I disbelieved, until I walked past that one in Czechoslovakia.

At Theresienstadt, we saw starvation and crazed desperation on the faces of those who chased us to tear at our clothing, yet none of us stopped to inspect conditions inside that camp.

It is hard, even now, to imagine. My only thought then was to run away from that frantic woman who pulled on my hair and grabbed off my jacket.

As for the SS officers on trial that day, I empathized with the ones who claimed to have been just following orders.

Truthfully, I thought the trial quite dull and tiresome. On and on droning lawyers questioned, translators translated, defendants responded, translators translated. An attorney rephrased the same question, drilling over and over, and the routine continued, dragging the process on and on. Throughout it all, the officers sat stoic.

Aware that it was a Big Event, I was nevertheless bored.

I was young—and ready to move on.

VII. Moving On—To the American Zone

After my return to Olpe and the Königs, I announced that I wanted to leave for Frankfurt, the Big City where the Americans were.

Even though I enjoyed my friends and the organizations I had joined, I still considered Olpe a tiny town of hypocrites.

Annelies had broken up with her fiancé and moved to Frankfurt to stay with her aunt. Eva Brinck had, at first, lived with the same lady, but now had her own room and offered to share her bed. She had written me: "Hannchen, come!"

Yes! But first, I must take one more trip to Gartrop to see Omi and Opa. I wrote in my little book: "Again this is very joyous, if it only didn't take two hours to get there on foot."

On March 21st, I did my last duty for the Königs by returning little 7-year-old Roland Bretschneider to Göttingen, so he could get back to the East Zone and his parents.

Suddenly, right after I returned, I got a very high fever and had to go to the hospital with chicken pox. During my four-week recuperation, three other women were in my room, but we never got acquainted. I did nothing but sleep. In the middle of a conversation, I would conk out again. My fever simply refused to go down. Both Mrs. Brinck and Mrs. König bravely came to visit me occasionally.

During a wake-up session, I inscribed in my notebook: "I will have to get better so I can move to Frankfurt/Main,* where Eva is."

Finally, I was well enough to travel to Frankfurt.

With permission of her landlady, Eva and I shared a bed. After resting a couple of days, I ventured out to find the Rhein/Main Airport, by then the headquarters of the US Air Force in Germany. The Americans needed workers who could speak English.

* As Germany has two Frankfurts, the city in Hessen on the Main River is known as Frankfurt am Main. A small town, Frankfurt an der Oder, is on the Polish border.

Although April, unseasonable heat caused everyone to wear summer clothes. With great hope, I rushed out to grab a streetcar headed in that general direction. From the last stop, I caught a train to the airport and then had to figure out where, in that huge complex, the personnel office might be. It was in a barracks near the airport drop-off entrance close to the autobahn and just a short walk (a mile) from the train station.

I still had the pocks on my face, but I was hired at once as a typist for the Civilian Personnel Office. My job was to interview and fill out forms about the people who had recently been hired.

My memory for their ID numbers took me by surprise. When I saw one of our new employees elsewhere, I would recognize him by his ID number, not necessarily his name. Generally, the men worked on airplanes; women cleaned buildings. Soon Eva got a job there, too, as an administrator.

What was best about my new job was not the money. It was a whole tray full of tasty food every day at lunchtime. For two weeks, my head had been aching, probably from hunger. Aspirin after aspirin did no good. Even with no breakfast, those mess hall treats—meats, veggies, rolls, pudding or cake—were Heaven! My favorite, something I had never seen or tasted before: canned peaches, golden juicy sweet ones. At night, I used my ration card to have a second meal, sometimes with some bread saved from my tray.

Early in my employment, another typist and I were sent to register a whole battalion of Latvians, who served as airport security guards. Their camp was only a streetcar ride from where I lived, and, during that four weeks, I enjoyed learning about those soldiers in black uniforms. Several of them told me they were of East Indian descent.

When I saw Eva's family photos in her room, I fervently missed my own. My intention had been to carry our albums on my flight from the Russians, but I had inadvertently left them at the Hitler Youth camp. A few others had been stashed in my little red book that was stolen in our Hamburg quarters.

I asked, and both Papi and Kiki loaned me the few they had saved. My father's favorites were of himself posing with his dogs and his cars. I offered to get duplicates made for each of us.

I found out that my childhood friend, Susie Peters had a cousin who owned a drugstore with a camera department in the Russian Zone. I contacted him by mail, and he responded that it would cost 350 Marks, which I agreed to pay. I sent him our family photos and asked that he make multiple copies.

Then our government devalued our money by 90% and issued new Deutsche Marks (DMs). We could turn in 10 Marks for one DM. Our salaries would stay the same, but we would be paid in DMs not Reichsmarks. Every person in Western Germany received 75 DMs in addition to their salary that one week to help them make the adjustment. Susie's cousin expected 350 DMs. I had no savings.

"I don't have it," I wrote back. "Please return my photographs."

He never did. It broke my heart. To my dad, that was one more tragedy. Never mind photos of the family, he mourned the loss of the ones with his prize-winning boxers and those coveted automobiles.

Eva Brinck.
Frankfurt. 1948.

After three months, Eva's bed seemed to get smaller, so Annelies's aunt helped me find a temporary room in a house next door to her. While I was staying there, I walked over to the aunt's house for a visit, when Billy, a friend of Eva's, stopped by and asked, "Where's Eva?"

I told him I did not know.

A tall, very respectable GI, whom Eva knew at her workplace, he struck up a conversation with me and added, "Let's walk awhile, and I'll buy you a cup of coffee."

Glancing down at my knee socks and clunker shoes, I almost refused.

In my hands, I was carrying a pair of stockings, a wooden darner, darning needle and scissors. I stuffed them into a deep pocket and agreed.

After a pleasant interlude at an American cafeteria, Billy and I window-shopped until I grew tired. Graciously, he called a cab, paid the driver and thanked me for joining him. But before the taxi driver could pull away from the curb, a policeman jerked open the door, grabbed me, dragged me out of the cab and made me climb up into a police van.

The next thing I knew, I was standing near a wall with multiple prostitutes in a police station. I wanted to die! I stood like a stick, not touching anything or anyone.

The policeman assigned to interrogate me soon realized I did not belong there. I wore no crazy makeup and looked very plain. He listened to my explanation and went to the office to confer with the others. I was released but had to walk all the way home.

When I arrived, there was a frantic Billy, trying to explain to Annelies's aunt what had happened. Unable to speak German, he had quickly disappeared, knowing the police would not believe him anyway.

Soon after that, I found another room two blocks away from Eva's and across the street from a bombed-out apartment house that was nothing but rubble. Unfortunately, the only place I could get was in the two-bedroom apartment of some low-class "scums."

The parents went to work every day, but their young adult daughter did not need a job, for her black boyfriend, an American soldier, "kept her up." The daughter was the boss. Her one-eyed father had nothing to say. As soon as he would leave in the morning, a man who worked with the mother would come in for coffee and who-knows-what with her.

I rented one of the two tiny bedrooms. The daughter slept on the living room sofa. All of us had to share a bathroom, a half-story down, with other families.

Because that bathroom had no shower or tub, we had to bathe at a public bath house. On Saturday afternoons, I would be standing in a line with other dirty neighbors, awaiting my turn in a tub. At least, the attendants scrubbed the tubs after each customer. On other days, I would have to wash up in that vulgar family's kitchen.

Only once did I actually appreciate the kindness of the mother of that household. In the middle of the night, I awoke screaming in pain. She came in, saw that I had no firewood for my tiny wood stove and soon returned to build a fire. Then she brought me a cup of tea, which made me feel better.

Apparently, my suffering was caused by a kidney stone, which soon passed.

That did not make up for the loss of my coat lined with Mami's ocelot fur, which had been stored in the basement. The mother shrugged. "Oh, it's gone, and we can't find it."

True, my wrap, my bed, my tent had become tattered and dirty, but to me, it was more than a coat. My mother enfolded me every time I pulled it around me.

Believe it or not, I did not miss the hiking, poetry and ping pong clubs nor even our traveling choir in Olpe. Frankfurt am Main offered far more opportunities to enjoy life, such as operas, plays, concerts of every variety and sidewalk cafes. Cozier cafes on a second floor offered tea, sweets and a view of activities below on the street. Eva and I got a kick out of walking arm-in-arm, like sisters, window-shopping at so many of the high-class shops and drooling.

With more than a half-million population, Frankfurt was a trading and banking center on the Lower Main River with a proud history dating back to the 9th Century. Medieval buildings and a tourist favorite, the Römer, also called Rathaus (city hall), contrasted to the modernistic railroad station with a unique half-circle glass entrance.

It was known as a "head station," that is, if a train came in from the north and was headed south, it would have to back way back to the north and then turn onto a south track.

That station, frankly, made me feel a bit creepy, for it was always crammed with prostitutes and foreigners with faces and languages unrecognizable to Germans. I could not help wondering if those Arab bandits had smuggled themselves in.

As for fun, Eva, Annelies and I met here and there and hung out together when not working, but my social life was not as varied as in Olpe. Both of them showed no shyness among men. Eva's Nordic good looks and ease when conversing with the opposite sex made me feel like a "pumpernickel nanny." I sort of held back, although, like my father, I loved to dance.

Our favorite "sport" was what I called "Schunkeln." On the other side of the river from the financial center was the old section of the city, Sachsenhausen, where streets were lined with pubs famous for apple wine. There, we would sip the wine and soon be linking arms with stranger, relative, neighbor, whoever, dancing and singing like one big family. Still arm-in-arm, we would climb on chairs and dance some more.

For awhile, I enjoyed the company of a German fellow, Hans Rudolph Zeier, a law student at Mainz University, who lived in a pleasant suburb of Frankfurt. After a visit to the zoo and a walk or two in one of the exquisite botanical parks, we drifted away from each other's company.

In the late summer of 1948, we got word from Omi that Opa had developed an infection around the gold plate implant for his dentures. He was hospitalized in a ward for underprivileged and homeless people. There it was discovered that he had cancer of the tongue. Part of it was cut out. Omi, who was by then 77, walked two hours every day to visit him in the hospital. There was little hope for his survival after they removed the entire tongue.

Poor Opa. Many years ago, when I was young, his bronchial asthma became so life-threatening that he had to go on oxygen. He was given last rites three times, but returned to good health. Now, his situation was far more miserable. Was he getting the quality of care our private doctors would have given? Of course not. Would he even have the opportunity to get last rites? Who knows? Our worries became more intense than when we had lost contact with them after the war.

While attending his funeral that fall, I looked across the graveyard and locked eyes with my father, who had come in from Cuxhaven. He seemed to be staring at a daughter he barely recognized. True, I no longer looked like a refuge, but I was not a fashion model, either. As we walked side-by-side across the flat barren terrain, Papi made some comment like, "I can just imagine one guy giving the door handle to the next guy, when he comes in." Perhaps he meant it as a compliment, but I took it as questioning my virginity. I loved my father, but I never forgave him for assuming I imitated his current wife.

One morning after my landlords had left, I heard a knock, knock on the door. When I opened it, there stood two tired bums who had hitchhiked from Cuxhaven and been dropped by a truck driver in front of our apartment house. One was my father; the other, his neighbor Eugen, who lived in their barracks but originally came from East Prussia. They wanted me to take them to seek work at the airport.

Eugen, his wife Annie and their little girl had been among the lucky ones who had fled the Russians. Many other East Prussians as well as Latvians, Lithuanians and Estonians had boarded ships of all descriptions to get out before the war ended. Those bombed ships still lie at the bottom of the Baltic Sea, known then as a cesspool, because of all the oil and "yuck" floating on the surface.

Whether my influence had anything to do with their getting a job I will never know, but those two looked like they needed work. They were hired to clean airplanes on the inside, sometimes on the night shift. What a job for this proud man! But we were together—and that was very important.

Well, we did not *live* together. He and Eugen were given quarters in a barracks especially for workers. Their beds were cots with straw mattresses, but they, too, delighted in trips to the mess hall.

Soon, I invited Kiki, who wanted desperately to get away from our stepmother, to come try for a job in our complex. Sure enough, she got one cleaning the BOQ (bachelor officers' quarters). As a young girl, my sister did not like her vulnerability among single men far from home. She applied and got a typing position. Luckily, she had found a place to live near the airport and a bicycle to get her back and forth.

The couple who took her in had lost their only son during the war and treated her as an adopted daughter.

At the Rhein/Main Airport, the Berlin Airlift was underway. The purpose: to deliver coal, food and other supplies to West Berliners, after Russia blockaded the supply lines from the Allied sections. Airplanes took off from our runways every two minutes for months, and there was never an accident.

Papi (2nd from right) and co-workers.
Rhein/Main Airport. 1948.

During this time, Americans donated handkerchiefs and chocolate bars for the children in Berlin. The idea came from an American pilot, Gail Halverson, whom everyone called The Candy Bomber. This was known as the "little airlift."

I volunteered to help make the handkerchief parachutes. We tied a string onto each corner of the handkerchief and then a Hershey or Nestle bar onto the end of the knotted strings. For this we got a meal. During one of those after-work sessions in January of 1949, Eva and I noticed that an Air Force sergeant stood nearby, eyeing me and smiling shyly.

Soon, he and I were snacking on cookies and drinking Coca-Cola on the premises. That soft drink always made me a bit dizzy, but perhaps that feeling was enhanced by clean-cut Charlie with the cute little nose and thick eyebrows almost hiding his soft blue eyes. Sergeant Charles Cotter had just been transferred to Rhein/Main for duty as a communications special-ist. From a tower overlooking the airfield, he sent and received Morse code messages.

During that first conversation, we discovered our mutual love of classical music, and we bonded. I knew instantly that I was in love with this handsome Boston Irishman. Even his name attracted me: Cotter sounded like the German Kotter.

He said he had re-enlisted because his wife was divorcing him to marry someone else, taking their daughters, Maureen, 9, and Patsy, 8, with her. Stepdaughters: fine with me!

Then he told me (and everyone else) what I knew would please my family. "I studied medicine."

Of course! This brilliant walking dictionary has great potential! But... "So why did you drop out of med school?"

"My wife insisted on it."

Not until 25 years later did I learn the truth. Long before his first marriage, he dropped out of the eighth grade!

Meanwhile, I was smitten. Our favorite dates were to attend concerts or just stop by a cafe or pub with music.

I never got to introduce him to the apple wine "Schunkelns." As a GI, he would have been uneasy in exclusively ethnic German surroundings.

Most Germans are known for their thirst for good beer. Not me. Apple wine topped beer because of the fun associated with it.

Charlie tried to introduce me to smoking. "That's what American girls do," he urged.

I tried a few cigarettes but I didn't like them. My addiction was to music.

One day when he picked me up from work, Charlie announced, "I have to show you what I've found!"

He hustled me downtown to an antique shop. My soulmate picked up an ebony and pewter flute, fingered it, put it to his mouth and played so beautifully that I fell even deeper in love. To be trite, I knew then that we could make beautiful music together—literally.

Despite all of this, whenever I went out in public with Charlie in uniform, I felt guilty. Frankly, I hated to see German girls running around with our former enemies, the Amis or Limeys. Never would I want to be known as one of those derisively nicknamed "Ami Liebchen" (American lovers)! I was uneasy even walking down the street beside a GI.

135

Charlie posing in a botanical garden. Frankfurt. 1949.

That's why, when riding the streetcar with him, I stood some distance away. Charlie seemed to be very understanding and gracious about this. Many other allied servicemen dated my peers, so, for him, there was no stigma.

The Americans originally ordered their troops not to fraternize during occupation, but when that seemed to be an unenforceable rule, they announced that, in the spirit of reconciliation and friendship, it would be okay.

By 1946, marriage to German nationals was allowed.

Papi's reaction to my dating an American was positive: he liked Charlie. Working for ones we used to call "the enemy," he had gotten to know some and respected them as normal human beings.

Even though being in the same airport complex with my new love, I found a better job as an interpreter with the architectural firm, Baurat Bischof, named for the key architect. As the German economy had improved, I no longer needed that big tray of food.

As I have always admired design and color and loved to draw, I had considered three careers during my teenage years.

First, I wanted to be a fashion designer.

"No, no," my dad had warned. "You'll be picking up pins the first three years."

Well then, maybe I could help other people. I would work for the Red Cross, reading mail and writing letters for soldiers.

Papi grimaced. "And emptying midnight vases."

Ugh, that was the German term for bedpans. I surely did not want to do that.

In my late teens, I had a better idea. I could take interior architecture at the famous Lettehaus in Berlin. My father's only objection? He could no longer afford to pay for tuition. Besides, no one knew when or how the war would end or what our circumstances might be.

Now, at my new job, I might learn about that trade, as I translated their communications.

Herr Bischof focused on the American and French Zones (Southwest Germany, near the Black Forest). At that time, he was designing houses for families of American GIs.

At the architectural firm, I enjoyed working with all the staff, but I found one architect particularly interesting, as he was from Breslau.

"Where did you live?" I asked.

Mr. Seidel glanced at me through thick glasses. "Victoriastrasse."

No, it couldn't be! That's where the upscale apartment house my father owned was located. That was the one occupied mostly by the wealthiest Jews in the city. But this guy was not of that faith. I was curious. "What number?"

"Twenty."

What a tiny world we live in!

Bischof Architectural Firm party. Mr. Seidel seated, hand on chin. Back: Hanna, 1st; Mr. Bischof, 4th. Christmas, 1951.

Sometimes, I would have to travel with my boss and one of his architects in his Opel Admiral.

Charlie did not like that one bit. Silly, Mr. Bischof was a grandfather, although another architect did travel with us. Charlie's main complaint was that they were taking me away from him. He also may not have approved of my forays across the river to "Schunkeln" either, but then he told me that would not be his kind of fun.

Frankly, I knew that he would not be comfortable there in his uniform. I enjoyed those outings with my architect friends, because it changed our formal relationships, if but for a few hours of Brüderschaft (brotherhood). At the office, we used the term Sie (translated you, the way one would address a boss, co-workers or strangers). But when partying at a pub, a male and female would link arms, take a swallow from a mug, kiss and say "Du" (you, used to address dear friends, relatives or a lover). The next day, I would become Fraulein Skiebe and Sie, and he was then Sie or Herr Whatever.

Meanwhile, Eva kept hinting that Charlie and I should get engaged.

My father, who treated Charlie as a friend, had some serious reservations. He lectured me until four o'clock in the morning, passing on his misgivings about our future: "Charlie is nice but not for you," indicating that my boyfriend did not have enough ambition or an important enough position in life.

In reply, I defended my Charlie, making him sound more important, more prestigious than he really was.

Not only did we have so much in common, this fellow was extraordinarily handsome in his new navy blue Air Force uniform with the light blue shirt and dark tie that he had traded for the khaki one worn by the Army Air Corps (which had become the US Air Force, a separate branch of service in 1947).

If Charlie asked my dad for my hand, I was unaware of the occasion. He never formally asked me. We just *knew*, and one day, we entered a jewelry store to select our rings: two gold ones just alike but different sizes. He slipped mine on my left ring finger.

In Germany, when engaged, each one wears a simple gold band on the left hand. That same ring goes on the right hand at the wedding.

Mine fulfilled my sweetest dreams, and I wanted the world to see it. On a streetcar, I would fling my hand around as though to say, "See my million dollar trophy?!"

Hanna and her beloved Charlie. Bavaria. 1950.

VIII. I Married an Enemy

Usually, when Charlie and I dated, frugality was the rule. Our paychecks were so small that sometimes Charlie would buy a pound of coffee at the commissary and sell it to a grateful German, who never received coffee rations and was willing to pay good money. (What was called "coffee" then was roasted wheat. Yuck!)

With plenty of parks to choose from, we did a lot of walking and talking, hand-holding and cheek-touching. Even window-shopping was fun with so many streets and shops to explore.

Only once did we splurge. Charlie and I took off a weekend to go skiing in Bavaria. We had no money for hotel accommodations, but Billa's family was kind about sharing their two rooms over a cow stable with us. Their son Peter and his sisters, Uschi and Renate, treated us like close relatives.

All day, my GI and I traversed up and down, up and down the slopes. That afternoon, the sun dipped behind the mountain we were on, and the top layer of snow quickly became ice. I wanted to make one more run. On the way down, I slipped and fell, cutting my face into slithers.

When I got back to work that Monday, people were asking, "What did Charlie do to you?"

The more I dated Charlie, the less I saw of my friends and family, although I tried to keep in touch with Papi, Kiki and Omi.

Albert, Charlie, Uschi, Renate, Billa and Peter (behind). Viechtach. 1951.

141

Fun in Frankfurt—with a friendly bear! 1950.

Eventually, Papi was able to get quarters in Mörfelden, a town outside of Frankfurt, where he could reunite his family. He, Käthe, Trautel and Omi moved into two attic rooms.

Their tight quarters must have put strains on their marriage, but Papi never complained.

Omi's life may have been even harder than before, because our mean stepmother used to treat her badly. Omi became her personal slave—cooking, cleaning, baby-sitting, whatever, while Käthe sat there smoking and shouting orders. Despite her "diet" of cigarettes, she grew fatter and fatter.

Our grandmother seemed to grow thinner. And what about my dad? He did not say anything about it, and she was the mother he loved so much!

While in Mörfelden, Papi and Käthe applied to get housing especially for refugees at a development in Waldorf. The terms required that prospective tenants do 600 hours of manual labor to build the project. Both also had to work to earn a down payment and rent money. At first, Käthe got a job at the airport cleaning the BOQ, but not long after that became a time sheet keeper. Trautel stayed with Omi when not in school.

When the others were out of the apartment, Omi read the newspaper from A to Z and wrote letters to every family member and old friend for whom she had an address. She became our link to those from our past.

Probably the only bright spot in Omi's dull days was a neighbor who lived upstairs in another attic room. A baroness from East Prussia, whose life had taken a drastic turn as well, saw Omi's unhappy predicament and recognized her as one with whom she shared circumstances.

She had heard the orders from Käthe's big mouth to the household slave, and her heart went out to Omi. This sweet neighbor became a friend so dear that she presented my grandmother with a precious Russian cross.

It must have been difficult for our grandmother to leave her only friend, and, once again, relocate.

But for my parents, their new apartment in Waldorf was worth the struggle. Four solidly built brick buildings had been constructed and connected, with four apartments each. Every building had its own entrance, and our family's freshly painted four-room apartment was downstairs. A strip of land for a garden was designated for each family.

Their former neighbors, Eugen, his wife and daughter from Cuxhaven, moved upstairs.

And I moved in, too, although it meant that I would have to ride the train back into Frankfurt every day to work.

I got the smallest of the four rooms to myself. Omi and Trautel shared the other bedroom while Papi and Käthe slept on a pull-out sofa in the living room. Three steps outside of their well-equipped kitchen was their garden space, where Omi and our father loved to putter.

Why would I want to be in the same household with Käthe? Frankly, I could hardly wait to get away from the "scums" in Frankfurt, and my parents needed my rent money as well as Omi's pension to make ends meet. Unlike her attitude toward Kiki and Omi, my stepmother's demeanor with me was tolerable. She seemed to respect me as a working adult, who was engaged.

Meanwhile, Käthe continued her orders and verbal attacks on her sweet mother-in-law. Even Trautel, who in her mother's eyes could do no wrong, recognized the injustice. One evening, she interrupted her mother's bitching with, "If you don't stop that, I'm going to run away!"

LEFT: Kiki, Charlie and Hanna in the Skiebes' new home.
RIGHT: Charlie and Hanna. Waldorf. 1951.

Kiki, Papi and Hanna. Frankfurt. 1951.

On the Saturday night of a Frankfurt festival, Käthe went out and did not return until after dawn Sunday. When questioned, my stepmother yelled at us for showing concern and haughtily admitted, "I never loved him. I only married him for his money." Then she laughed like a witch.

That fit my longtime impression of her as a "gold digger."

Probably the only reason Käthe let Omi continue to live with them was her potential "wealth." The government announced that some restitution would be provided for families who had lost homes and other major assets after the war. In fact, more than half of the Marshall Plan funds were spent for reparations required by the plan. If a person could prove with deeds or several witnesses the ownership of property that had been confiscated, they could get 10% of the property value. Because the Mark had been devalued, that really meant about 1% of what it was worth. Even that amount for Omi would be significant. My dad could also prove he was due a hefty amount, compared to his annual salary. Meanwhile, he continued his menial job.

From their new apartment, Papi rode his bicycle to and from the airport. At midnight on a rainy evening, he was returning from work through the woods. The bicycle light worked only when he pedaled, so when the tires stopped in the mushy dirt, my father could not see around him, lost his balance, fell and cracked his skull. Determined not to die in the dark, he somehow dragged himself up, hung his shoulders over the handlebars, turned and laboriously made his way back to the airport, where someone called an ambulance.

As soon as we were notified, family members rushed to the hospital to learn that he not only suffered a concussion, but also had a broken nose. We thought he was going to die! To our amazement, he stayed in the hospital only four weeks and soon recuperated enough to get back to work.

When my employer asked me to go to a project at Augsburg in Bavaria for four weeks to replace an interpreter, Charlie's reaction was "Tell them to go to Hell!"

"No!" I insisted with equal firmness. "Four weeks is nothing. I need that job!"

That hot exchange put a kink in our relationship, but I followed orders—of my boss, that is.

Charlie saw me off at the train station. As he kissed me goodbye, I broke down sobbing. Once into the coach, I covered my head with my coat from embarrassment. It did not come off until I reached my destination.

Just by chance, as soon as I got to Augsburg, I ran into the parents of one of Kiki's former classmates. They allowed me to stay with them, although it might have been because they needed the rent money.

A night or two after I had arrived, I woke up yelling. Not because of a kidney stone. Because of Charlie. In my psyche, I knew something was horribly wrong.

Indeed it was. I got a call at the office the next day from a worker at our firm in Frankfurt. Headlines in the Frankfurt newspapers reported his arrest.

In short, Charlie had "gone bananas" about my leaving. He got drunk and was driving an Army jeep down a main street next to the streetcar line. At a crosswalk, where riders disembark and move across the street to the sidewalk, vehicles are supposed to stop. He not only disobeyed the law, he knocked down a girl and ran over her leg. So drunk he didn't realize what happened, he continued a block farther before stopping.

The authorities were angry. Until then, incidents involving German civilians often went unreported. This time, the occupying forces decided to prosecute publicly. His was the first trial publicized to show how Americans take care of such tragedies and the victim involved.

At the military trial, he was sentenced to two weeks in the brig, and the young woman's medical bills were paid, with more compensation for pain and suffering.

I was humiliated. That was my Charlie in the brig—because of *me!* Not only that, he was demoted from sergeant to private, and the story was not only published in the Frankfurt newspapers but also the military's *Stars and Stripes.*

My father again expressed his doubts about my marrying this guy, but I defended Charlie with my whole heart.

Our plans did not change. Charlie and I would marry soon after Kiki and I were settled in America and Charlie could get transferred back to the States.

Within a short time, I was filling out all the papers to go to the United States. I did not have the proper stamps to mail them, and it was not until Kiki later applied for a visa that I remembered what I had forgotten to do. I nearly had heart failure! We had already been to a travel agency to book the trip. *What if...?* I immediately put them in the mail, barely in time.

When the Big Day arrived, Charlie was on duty and could not see me off to Paris, but Dad and Käthe put my sister and me on the night train for our first leg of the trip. Our father expressed how happy he was for us, but I detected a concern for our well-being, too.

Had we not been so excited about our final destination, Paris would have been even more exhilarating! But Kiki and I tried to see it all in one day: the Avenue des Champs Elysées, Arc de Triomphe, Eiffel Tower, St. Madeleine Church, Notre Dame and the Seine. Unfortunately, the Louvre was closed that day, but we kept walking, gazing, marveling until our feet and stomachs hurt.

Kiki relied on me to communicate, for she knew I had taken French six years in school. But I feared that no one would understand me and never tried. By suppertime, we stopped in a bakery, where I pointed at some muffins. The clerk smiled, made change and gave us our sweet dinner.

Hanna at the Arc de Triomphe. Paris, France. January, 1952.

At the rather antiquated hotel with simplistic rooms and a bathroom down the hall, we pretended to be Americans, speaking English to the staff. As we finished paying and signing out, the manager tilted his head and grinned. "Auf Wiedersehen, Fräulein, ich hoffe dass Sie gut in Amerika ankommen." ("Good-bye, ladies. Have a good trip to America.")

The next morning, we had to rise at dawn to ride the metro to the station where we would board the train for Le Havre. At both the metro and railroad stations, couples were "kanoodling" and kissing after a long night.

Finally, the ship I had imagined ever since my mother had crossed the Atlantic on it loomed above us, as we stood on the dock. The old S.S. Europa had been bought and refurbished by France. Now it was the gleaming S.S. Liberté. Mami, Papi, Billa, Kiki and I had cruised the Baltic Sea on ships and fishing vessels every summer vacation, but this one surpassed all of those in size and elegance.

As the ocean liner backed away from the pier on my "lucky" day (January 26th), I delighted in the anticipation of living out two dreams—to get to America and to marry my beloved!

Simultaneously, I mourned leaving friends behind. My whole young life had been a cycle of making friends, leaving them behind, making new ones and leaving them, again and again. *Would that continue?*

More questions quelled my excitement. *Would Charlie's mother like me? Would a German be accepted? How dramatically would my life change?*

Then the thrill overwhelmed me. *Here we go! America, here we come!*

As we entered our tourist class inside cabin, Kiki gleefully leapt to the top bunk like the gymnast that she was.

Had we not enjoyed brief friendships with fellow passengers, our cruise-of-a-lifetime would have been horribly marred by a ferocious winter storm with monstrous waves. No one was allowed on the icy decks, but we got to know fascinating people from European countries, including Germany, headed to New York—not as tourists but, like us, as immigrants.

Near the end of our trip on the elegantly renovated S.S. Liberté, I, too, succumbed to seasickness. A man next to me threw up and I joined him.

The next day, my heart almost jumped out of my body. Right in front of me, the Statue of Liberty had burst into view! Tears ran down my cheeks. I looked around. Everyone in sight was crying, too.

How could I thank Onkel Josef for all that he had already done for Kiki and me? By sponsoring us to come to America, he gave us a new life. On our arrival, he would welcome us into his home until we could make it on our own. We were very grateful but well aware of why the family labeled him "Crazy Josef."

A native of Krotoczyn, Poland, Josef Piskorek served in the military during World War I. After the war, he established a deli in Kiel, then returned to Poland in the 1920s and opened a deli, then a fine restaurant with a bowling alley and park in Krotoczyn, then a hair salon in Posen.

He was doing so very well, he must have assumed that, if he could be successful there, surely he could do better in America. So he left his wife, daughter Sophie and son Kurt behind. He said he would send for them later.

Their young nanny, Antoinette, watched for the mail and got his address in Chicago, where he owned and operated a beauty salon. As soon as she could leave, he sent for her to join him. His children's nanny, now his mistress, was 22 years his junior.

When conditions in Poland worsened, Sophie, then a teenager, begged her father, "Please, let me come over!" Josef had compassion for his only daughter, so he sponsored her. Then Sophie pleaded for him to sponsor her mother and Kurt. Josef relented and they all lived together! Antoinette was still beautiful and bedecked with diamonds Josef had given her. His wife had grown heavy from unhappiness.

Around 1929, he joined the Beethoven Society (a German-American social group) in Chicago. One night, the family attended a meeting, except for Josef and Antoinette. When the others returned home, they discovered the place empty.

Josef and his mistress had moved to New York to

establish a salon there. A divorce followed.

In 1936, he returned to Germany with Antoinette, his new bride, for the 1936 Olympics and to visit their families in Poland and us in Breslau.

By the time I got to New York, Josef had changed his name twice. From Piskorek, he became Kovac in Chicago. By 1952, he was a Seiler (pronounced Zyler).

Onkel Josef was nowhere in sight on Pier 86, but Kiki and I spotted Antoinette and another woman waving at us. We waited for our name to be called and papers checked, so we could greet them.

Irish immigration officers in dark blue uniforms had boarded to conduct the process. Kiki and I tried to be patient, but our name must have been last. My favorite passenger friend was leaving, and I rushed to tell her goodbye, but one of the officers, a middle-aged bully, physically stopped me. His words and man-handling were not too welcoming, but I waited until his attention had turned to someone else and sneaked close enough to her to wish her well.

All passengers had been processed, and we were still standing on the deck. Leftovers.

"Did we call you?" the uniformed bully asked.

I shook my head. "No."

"What's your name?"

"Skiebe (pronounced Skeebeh)."

"I called Skiebe (pronounced Sky´bee)!"

Neither Kiki nor I argued. We were ready to set foot on that American dock and run into our future.

Our aunt and her friend welcomed us with hugs and kisses and hurried our luggage into Antoinette's fashionable Oldsmobile for the ride to the Seiler home in Flushing.

Kiki craned her neck to peer up at the skyscrapers of Manhattan, and I kept glancing at landmarks I had seen only in photographs, while trying not to be rude to the ladies and their constant conversation. As we traveled through busy, busy streets, lights began popping on, changing dusk into night.

No apartment was good enough for our uncle and aunt, who each flashed seven-carat yellow diamonds on their ring fingers. Their stucco and brick Tudor home and garage sat in a well-kept yard, with a garden and grass not quite green yet after a winter of snow.

When Antoinette opened the front door, welcoming shouts came from Onkel Josef and a houseful of guests, including some of Antoinette's relatives and a German couple who lived across the street.

Surrounded by noisy strangers hugging and kissing us like family, Kiki and I were stunned. In our culture, such people would be shaking hands.

After the excitement was over and guests were gone, our proud uncle took on an officer's tone when he frowned and barked, "You *lied* to me!"

"About what?"

He pointed to the gold band on my left hand. "You said you were not married."

"I'm not. Not yet." I tried to remind him that, in Germany, we wear the band on our left hand when engaged, the right when married.

He definitely did not want to hear that. Pacing like a major general, my uncle admitted rather pompously that he had other plans. He had personally selected one of the sons of his German friends to be my husband.

I told him about Charlie and our plans to marry as soon as he could get back to the States.

When his tone softened with the realization that he could not control me as he did others in his life, I saw him as more eccentric than military, with Mami's family's red hair just on top and shaved skin where gray had likely been on his temples.

Immediately, Kiki and I were enthralled by the first television we had ever seen: a moving picture coming from somewhere else with unheard-of shows! It was in a basement room with a bar, microphone, and piano—a great party place.

Our next days were more relaxed until the third one, when Antoinette, flashily dressed to match her yellow diamond, escorted us to Manhattan to get social security cards. After a long wait in line, Kiki and I were ready to find employment. From there, Antoinette took us to check by the unemployment office to see what jobs were available and then to find the addresses for our interviews.

My first interview yielded a typing job at the corporate office of a company that manufactured men's blazers. I was to start the following Monday. Kiki got a job as a typist, too, but not in the same part of Manhattan as mine.

That first time we were on our own to get to work, my sister and I had to walk to find the right bus to town, then the right subway, change at the right subway stop and then, in my case, walk along Fifth Avenue to 28th Street.

Never having seen American money, we puzzled over what coins to use for the bus, the subway or a snack. We had to figure out what a dime looked like and how much it was worth in our own culture.

At work, I hesitated to open my mouth for fear that my co-workers would hear my accent. I worried that several of the secretaries, administrators, file clerks and other typists who were Jewish would assume that I had killed someone during the war.

On Fridays, the other girls quickly took off at lunchtime to spend their paychecks, returning with big bags of bargain clothes. I shopped more carefully for my wedding outfit.

Our uncle, now in his 60s, had sold all of his beauty salons but one 20 minutes away in Corona. He and Antoinette, a hairdresser, went there every day. On Fridays, he invited Kiki and me to come for "the works."

My first Friday in the USA, he insisted that I get a permanent. I had just gotten one in preparation for my trip. No matter, I must have another. Suddenly, my medium-length hair was shorter and unbecomingly kinky. Kiki's became a blonde fuzz ball. Despite my intense reaction to my mother's bright red nails when she returned from Onkel Josef's care, I did not have the guts to protest getting red nails on my fingers *and* toes.

Our uncle and aunt wanted to do everything possible for us. I could not be rude nor unappreciative.

But I knew his reputation for wanting to control everyone in sight.

His father had died after Josef came to America, so years later, when he had made his fortune, he returned to visit his father's grave. A nice headstone for him had been placed in the cemetery, but pompous Josef had it replaced by a much

153

taller finer one, with beautiful lettering. At the base, it read: "Donated by his son Josef."

At the end of March, my Charlie arrived. In contrast to his anger that I was engaged, Onkel Josef invited Charlie to stay in an extra room at their house.

My meticulous aunt and uncle were charmed by my fiancé in his Air Force uniform with the gleaming belt buckle, visor on his cap and shoes, all shined to perfection. Perhaps he reminded them, too, of a dark-haired Henry Fonda.

The plan was to visit Charlie's mom in Somerville, Massachusetts (just outside of Boston) for the weekend and return to Flushing, so that we could be married March 31st, a Monday. Then I would continue working until I had enough money for the railroad trip to join him at his next duty station in Oklahoma City.

Mrs. Cotter greeted me so cordially, I immediately felt that she liked me. Within a very few minutes, she excused herself and led Charlie to another room, where she bawled him out about something relating to his ex-wife and daughters, Maureen and Patsy. Once that was over, she politely returned to make me feel at home.

A widow, Annie Cotter revered and emulated her late husband, a parent who attended church regularly, never cursed and set a good example for his children. He died of heart disease in his 50s. I grew to love her deeply.

While in her two-story house with a porch around three sides, I saw where Charlie learned his fastidiousness, for her home was neatly arranged, with not one chair, piece of china or ashtray out of place.

One interesting fact I heard that day about the family I was marrying into: Charlie's great-grandmother's sister was Georgianna Drew Barrymore who bore the famous movie stars, John, Ethel and Lionel.

Because the Cotters were Catholic and Charlie was divorced, we would be married by a justice of the peace. We arranged to do it at New York state's Jamaica Courthouse and remain with the Seilers. During and after Charlie's furlough, I would continue working until the end of April, then I would follow him to Oklahoma. Thus, Charlie hung around the house, while the rest of us went to work.

In New York, I was amazed how generous people were. Not only did friendships come easy, but they gave and gave. On my last day of work before I was to marry, about ten of the girls at the office took me to a restaurant for lunch and handed me $25, so that I could pick out a wedding gift. I purchased an Indian vase, which I still treasure.

On our wedding day, Charlie and I, Kiki and Antoinette took a bus then a subway to the courthouse in Jamaica. When he handed the justice of the peace what he thought was his divorce papers, Charlie was shocked to find out he did not have the proper ones. He had to call the Boston Courthouse to discuss his dilemma. A clerk offered to send the appropriate papers by special delivery, so we could expect them to arrive the next morning.

When the four of us reappeared at the Jamaica Courthouse on April Fool's Day, Kiki, my maid of honor, announced, "You'd better get married today. I'm not going to take another day off."

Charlie and Hanna Cotter. Jamaica, NY. April 1, 1952.

And so, in my new navy suit with horizontal stripes on the jacket and a matching navy hat and high-heeled shoes, I stood ready to say the vows.

My white corsage, presented to me by my co-workers at the luncheon, matched my fancy sheer nylon blouse with the tiny tucks down the front.

With my aunt, Antoinette, as our other witness, Charlie and I repeated after the officiator and placed each other's ring back on the left hand, according to American custom.

Our "reception" was orchestrated by Antoinette with her usual flair and finances. First, the four of us hopped a subway to

155

Radio City Music Hall, where we watched the Rockettes strut and kick and dance in a perfect line, then settled down to see the movie "Singing in the Rain." From there, we took another subway to 86th Street and the German section.

At Cafe Geiger, we sipped coffee and devoured dreamy tortes. After exploring the German section, we ended the evening in the Brauhaus, where they brewed their own brand of beer, served German specialties and featured "oompah" music and dancing.

Someone, probably my talkative aunt, tipped off the announcer that Charlie and I were newlyweds, bringing many congratulations—and, for me, much embarrassment.

Our romantic first night concluded in his room in the Seilers' home.

Our "honeymoon" was not in the Big City. Charlie and I walked arm-in-arm to a corner drugstore, where we sat at the counter and savored ice cream sundaes, a new treat for me, for I was more used to a less-creamy Italian ice.

As we spooned our dessert, we gazed eye-to-eye into our future.

I felt so lucky that my dream had become reality. How could I have ever imagined this? Just a few years ago, I was incredibly lonely and struggling to survive.

Even today, I think back on those terrible times, and I thank God to be here in the most desirable, greatest country in the world, where I am an equal to others.

What would my life have been like if we didn't have that horrible war? Did the loss of my privileged life change *me* as well as my circumstances? Sure, and I definitely would not have married my Charlie—and would never have had my three wonderful sons, Tom, Robbie and Peter.

My traumatic flight from the Russians became a flight into a fantastic future!

Hanna Cotter. Washington, DC. 1953.

Lovey-Dovey: Charlie and Hanna. Washington, DC. 1953.

EPILOGUE

Charlie's military service took us to Tinker Air Force Base in Oklahoma and then Andrews Air Force Base near Washington DC, where I worked for the American Red Cross until he was discharged in late 1953.

Charlie worked for Republic Aviation in Long Island, NY, until 7,000 people were laid off in two weeks—just before our son Tom was born. This brought on an enormous hardship. Charlie was offered a temporary position at a US Post Office, but he had developed a rare eye condition and could not work, so as soon as I stopped nursing my baby, I took the job. Meanwhile, we had to find new quarters in an attic. Shortly afterward, Charlie got a job as an orderly in a mental hospital and I became a secretary at a factory, so that we could buy a small home.

As soon as I started working, I found myself pregnant. Seven months later, I left that job to deliver son #2, Robbie. That same year, 1956, I earned my citizenship. From then on, I stayed home until our son Peter was born seven years later.

In 1964, I took all three boys to Frankfurt to see my father to his delight. A brief time after we came home, Charlie lost his job, so I applied for the night shift at Brookhaven National Laboratory (which used to be a German POW camp), where I was a scanner in the physics department. We scanned atomic interactions and recorded the results into a huge computer with punch cards and tapes. I worked there for 11 years.

In 1975, after 23 years of marriage, Charlie and I went through a painful divorce. I started taking college evening classes while working in public relations for an architectural firm. A year or so later, I decided to go to Suffolk Community College full time, where I earned an associate's degree in 1980.

I got a full scholarship for the Southampton branch of Long Island University, where I earned my BFA. Not wanting to stop, I transferred to the C.W. Post campus of the same university for my Masters in Fine Art.

After 13 years of being single I married a quiet, good-natured man, my Buddy. John McCloskey's main interests are golf, carpentry and crossword puzzles. He encourages me in everything I do and is always supportive. My sons are very happy about this union.

Since 1989, Buddy and I have lived in North Carolina, where Tom enticed us to move. My oldest son, his wife Pat and son Brian have a home in Davidson, NC. Rob and Maureen live in Raleigh. Ian, their son attends Appalachian State University. Peter had bought my house on Long Island and still resides there. He presented us with a little girl, Sophie.

My lifelong interest in art has become my passion. While still on Long Island, I won awards and had several one-man shows. One of my oils, "The Green Sun," was critically acclaimed in the Arts section of *The New York Times*. In North Carolina, my paintings have been featured in galleries and art shows. According to a recent article, my work is in many private collections in the United States and Europe.

Had there been no war, would I have become an artist in Breslau? Probably.

Johanna's sons, Tom, 10, Robbie, 8, and Peter, 7 weeks.
Long Island, NY. 1963.

ABOVE: Naturalization Certificate for Hanna, by then Johanna Cotter. Suffolk County, NY. 1956. BELOW: Hanna's journal and Kiki's even smaller (2" x 2") one. 2005.

ILLUSTRATIONS

VII. Moving On—To the American Zone

VIII. I Married an Enemy

Epilogue

Index

Hanna Skiebe's Flight

1945	where	state/zone	how got there
January			
26	Lüben	Silesia	train
27	Haynau	" "	walked
28	Bunzlau	" "	walked
29?	Gorlitz	" "	walked
February			
6-17	Wigandsthal	" "	walked
17	Neustadt	" "	walked/train?
17	Friedland	Sudetenland	walked/train?
18	Bad Oppersdorf	" "	walked/train?
18	Zittau	" "	train
19	Hainewalde	Saxony	walked/train?
??	Rundstal	Sudetenland	walked/train
??	Alpacca	" "	train
28	Hohenelbe	" "	train
28-3/22	Spindelmühle	" "	train/bus/walked
March			
22-26	Habelschwerdt	Silesia	train
27-5/7	Spindelmühle	Sudetenland	train/walked
May			
7	Hohenelbe	" "	bicycle
8	Thannwald	" "	bicycle
8	30 km to Prague	Czech./RO	oil truck
8	Theriesenstadt	" "	walked
9	Leitmeritz	" "	walked
10?	Lobositz	" "	walked
10?	Aussig	" "	walked
11	Turmitz	" "	walked
??	Seestadel	" "	train
??	Görkau	" "	walked
??	Komatau	" "	train
19?	Chemnitz	Saxony/RZ	train
20-22	Braunsdorf	" " RZ	train/walked
22	Lichtenwald	Saxony/RZ-AO	walked
??	Cossen	" "	walked/train?
??	Ober-Gröfenhain	" "	walked
??	Jahnshain	" "	walked

RO=Russian occupied   AO=American Occupied

??	Altenburg	Thüringen/RZ-AO	walked
??	Zeitz	Saxony-Anhalt/RZ-AO	train
??	Theissen	" "	coal truck
??	Gotha	Thüringen/RZ-AO	coal train/walked
26	Eisenach	" "	walked?
29?	Braunhausen	Hessen/AZ	freight train
??	Heinebach	" "	train?
June			
1-3	Melsungen	" "	dairy truck/walk
5	Nielsungen	" "	truck/walked
6	Landwehrhagen	" "	walked
7-9	Hann-Münden	Lower Saxony/BZ	walked
10	Kassel	Hessen/AZ	train
12?	Siegen	Westphalia*/BZ	walked/freight car
13?	Finnentrop	" "	freight car
14-18	Bochum	" "	passenger train
19	Ahlen	" "	truck
20	Bielefeld	" "	cement truck
21	Herford	" "	truck
22	Hannover	Lower Saxony/BZ	2 coal cars
22	Harburg	Hamburg/BZ	baggage car
23-8/5	Hamburg	" "	auto
August			
5-11	Bochum	Westphalia*/BZ	passenger train
12-?	Olpe	" "	passenger train
25	Bochum	" "	passenger train
September			
??	Salzgitter	Lower Saxony/BZ	train
??	Elmshorn	Schleswig Holstein/BZ	train
25-10/9	Glückstadt	" "	walked?
October			
9	Elmshorn	" "	train
10	Hamburg	Hamburg/BZ	train
10	Osnabrück	Lower Saxony/BZ	coal car
10	Wanne-Eickel	Westphalia*/BZ	caboose
11	Hagen	" "	train
11	Finnentrop	" "	train
11	Olpe	" "	train

* North Rhine Westphalia

Kiki and Georg Skiebe's Flight

January-May   Kiki - refugee/work camp outside of Breslau
                  Georg - fighting in Breslau siege

May-October   Both lived with family but doing forced labor.

October

Date	Place	Region	
5-10	Freight car to Warsaw	Silesia/Poland	RZ
10	Forst	Brandenburg	RZ
11	Cottbus	" "	RZ
12	Torgau	Saxony	RZ
12	Halle	Saxony-Anhalt	RZ
13-14	Magdeburg	" "	RZ
15	Haldensleben	" "	RZ
15	Eilsleben	" "	RZ
16	Sommerschenburg	" "	RZ
16	Eilsleben	" "	RZ
17	Marienborn	" "	RZ
18	Helmstedt	Lower Saxony	BZ
19	Braunschweig	" "	BZ
20-21	Hamburg	Hamburg	BZ
22	Cuxhaven	Lower Saxony	BZ
25	Hamburg	Hamburg	BZ
November			
24	Glückstadt	Schleswig-Holstein	BZ
25-12/4	Cuxhaven	Lower Saxony	BZ
December			
5	Olpe	Westphalia*	BZ

* North Rhine Westphalia

INDEX
People and Places

Johanna steering a "Woody" with sons, Robbie, Tom and Peter during a Woody Party. Davidson, NC. 2003.

ORDER NOW FROM ABB!
True-experience stories and anecdotes, autographed:

__copies *Flight from the Russians*
       A German Teenager's World War II Ordeals
       Johanna Cotter McCloskey. Vintage photos and Index
       2005. 176 pp. ISBN: 1-893597-08-3
       Paperback @ $14.95 $_____

__copies *German War Child*
       Growing Up in World War II
       Christa Blum Mercer. Vintage photos and Index
       2004. 45 short stories. 176 pp. ISBN:1-893597-07-5
       Paperback @ $14.95 $_____

__ copies *World War II - Hometown and Home Front Heroes*
       Life-experience stories from the Carolinas' Piedmont
       77 authors and 23 contributors Vintage photos and Index
       2003. 115 stories. 320 pp. ISBN:1-893597-06-7
       2nd printing 2003. Paperback @ $17.95 $_____

__copies *The Great Depression - How We Coped, Worked and*
       Played Life-experience stories from the Carolinas' Piedmont
       65 authors Illustrated by Lexie Little Hill. Vintage photos and Index
       2001. 131 stories. 288 pp. ISBN:1-893597-04-0
       3rd printing 2002. Paperback @ $15.95 $_____

__copies *Gray-Haired Grins & Giggles*
       Guess what - Grandy & Grammy have a sense of humor, too!
       True tales from 45 authors. Cartoons by Loyd Dillon
       1995. 160 tales. 128 pp. ISBN:0-9640606-3-9
       4th pr. 1996. Paperback @ $12.95 Large print @ 13.95_____

__copies *World War II: It Changed Us Forever*
       From the battlefront to the homefront and places in between
       33 authors tell it like it was! Vintage photos and Index
       1994. 93 stories. 140 pp. ISBN:0-9640606-0-4
       3rd printing 2001. Paperback @ $12.95 $_____

Margaret Bigger's guide to recording memoirs:

__copies *Recalling Your Memories on Paper, Tape or Videotape*
       Self-help guide to preserving memoirs & photos. Also, how
       to assist relatives. Excerpts from seniors' family booklets.
       1996. Vintage photos 160 pp. ISBN:0-9640606-4-7
       2nd printing 2002 (revised). Paperback @ $13.95 $_____

Please complete the other side of this order form.

Collections of true humorous anecdotes:
Humor makes great gifts - autographed & personalized!!!

_copies *Churchgoers' Chuckles Vol. 2*
> True Tales - You Can't Make This Stuff Up! From 18 denom-
> inations in 25 states. Cartoons by Loyd Dillon
> 2005. 96 pp. ISBN 1-893597-09-1 Paperback @ $8.50 $_____

_copies *Advice Not Found in Wedding Guides*
> Great advice based on 20 years of collecting glitch stories.
> 2002. 128 pp. ISBN 1-893597-05-9 Paperback @ $9.95 $_____

_copies *MotherHoot - The Lighter Side of Motherhood*
> True anecdotes about moms from pregnancy through grandmotherhood
> + MotherHoot Tips for Sanity Cartoons by Loyd Dillon
> 1999. 128 pp. ISBN 0-9640606-8-X Paperback @ $9.95 $_____

_copies *DaddyHoot - The Lighter Side of Fatherhood*
> True anecdotes about dads from expectancy through grandfatherhood
> + DaddyrHoot Tips for Sanity   Cartoons by Loyd Dillon
> 2000. 112 pp. ISBN 0-9640606-9-8 Paperback @ $9.95 $_____

_copies *Kitties & All That Litter*
> Mewsings, GRRRoaners, true cat tales and kitty limericks
> by 26 cat-loving curmudgeons. Cat-tooned by Loyd Dillon
> 1999. 96 pp. ISBN 1-893597-00-8 Paperback @ $7.50 $_____

_copies *You've GOT to Have a Sense of Humor to*
> *Have a Wedding* Humorous, outrageous & disastrous true tales
> + advice not found in wedding guides. Cartoons by Loyd Dillon
> 1997. 128 pp. ISBN 0-9640606-5-5 Paperback @ $9.95 $_____

Subtotal $_____
Discount   **(20% for 10 or more)**
NC residents must add 7.5% tax $_____
Postage & handling $3.50 for 1st 2 books
              +$1 more for each multiple of 5 $_____

                    TOTAL $_____

Name_____   **Phone #**_____

Address_____

City, State, Zip_____

Mail check or money order to:
A. Borough Books 3901 Silver Bell Dr., Charlotte, NC 28211
    Specify HERE how you want your books to be personalized: